I0817606

A LONG GAME

ALSO BY ELIZABETH McCRACKEN

Here's Your Hat What's Your Hurry

The Giant's House

Niagara Falls All Over Again

An Exact Replica of a Figment of My Imagination

Thunderstruck & Other Stories

Bowlaway

The Souvenir Museum

The Hero of This Book

A LONG GAME

NOTES ON WRITING FICTION

ELIZABETH McCRACKEN

ecco
An Imprint of HarperCollins*Publishers*

 For information, address HarperCollins Publishers, 195 Broadway, New York, NY 10007. In Europe, HarperCollins Publishers, Macken House, 39/40 Mayor Street Upper, Dublin 1, D01 C9W8, Ireland.

hc.com

HarperCollins books may be purchased for educational, business, or sales promotional use. For information, please email the Special Markets Department at SPsales@harpercollins.com. harpercollins.com.

FIRST EDITION

Designed by Alison Bloomer

Library of Congress Cataloging-in-Publication Data

Names: McCracken, Elizabeth author
Title: A long game : notes on writing fiction / Elizabeth McCracken.
Description: First edition. | New York : Ecco, 2025. | Includes index.
Identifiers: LCCN 2025002636 (print) | LCCN 2025002637 (ebook) | ISBN 9780063375291 hardcover | ISBN 9780063375307 trade paperback | ISBN 9780063375314 ebook
Subjects: LCSH: Fiction—Authorship | Fiction—Technique
Classification: LCC PN3355 .M215 2025 (print) | LCC PN3355 (ebook) | DDC 808.3—dc23/eng/20250709
LC record available at https://lccn.loc.gov/2025002636
LC ebook record available at https://lccn.loc.gov/2025002637

25 26 27 28 29 LBC 6 5 4 3 2

A LONG GAME

I

1 | NOBODY KNOWS HOW TO WRITE A BOOK. NOBODY even knows how to start. Start at the start, says the wag.

2 | FOR MANY YEARS THE OPENING LINE OF A STORY OR novel was the first thing I knew, never changing through drafts, though everything else did: chronology, plot, setting, character. My ambition was to end up as an entry in *Bartlett's Familiar Quotations*. I used to be a librarian; I wanted to appear in a reference book.

That hasn't happened yet, so I've been forced to write my own.

3 | THIS IS A BOOK THAT DISPENSES ADVICE, COMposed by a writer of fiction. As with any such book or craft talk or social media rant or workshop critique, a lot of it is hogwash. I'm talking to myself. That's all writers really do. Give speeches to the mirror, whisper into a shell on the beach, find a stranger in a dive bar. Teach.

Eventually the odd writer is driven to write a book about writing. Craft books, these volumes are called: chipper, cheerleaderish, generally with an encouraging second-person narrator meant to make the whole exhausting process of writing a book seem possible. *You can do it!*

It's a reasonable stance: you'll never stand on the winner's podium if you can't get off the starting block.

But I don't know if you can write a book. I don't know if *I* can write a book. I don't know if I can write *this* book, though over the past thirty years I've published four novels, three collections of short stories, and a memoir, and have written several more unpublished books. (How many? We won't speak of that yet.) Everything that I have ever believed was true and immutable about my work has changed. Only certain obsessions remain. A writing life, I've come to believe, is a yearslong process of casting away everything you once believed for sure.

4 | I'M NOT SURE WHAT CRAFT MEANS WHEN IT COMES to writing fiction. How to think about the elements of fiction, perhaps, whatever an *element* is. Character, plot, setting, theme, structure, time, language, dialogue. (This isn't a complete list.) Of these, what's essential? Some fiction has no dialogue, or no defined setting—though maybe placelessness is itself a kind of setting. Language? There are word-free graphic novels that are undeniably fiction. No single element of fiction makes fiction fiction.

How do you separate such things anyway? Fiction isn't human anatomy, with a circulatory system separate from the skeleton, reproductive organs intertwined with but distinct from digestion. A piece of fiction isn't a human being, though it is human, or should be. It can't be all blood, or all bones, or all breath, or blood and bones and breath but no muscle to move. All bones and no spirit. All metaphor but no human will.

It would be useful to be able to map it, as the body is mapped in an anatomy book, with acetate transparencies so that you can lift away plot and leave character, lift away character and study tension, lower each and see it: the human hand, a human story.

5 | WHEN I WAS A CHILD, I HAD A BROWN BLANKET with a café au lait binding. The blanket itself was terrible, some late 1960s synthetic material that, by the time it came to me, had developed hard warts and polyps. I can't imagine that it was ever soft or pleasant; you could have grated cheese upon it. I didn't carry it around or name or anthropomorphize it in the security blanket tradition. I didn't love it, only the way it made me feel. The binding at the top was satin, also synthetic but silken, slippery—material can fail to accomplish things in one form and succeed in another; this, too, is a lesson of fiction—and I took enormous pleasure in running that binding across my top lip, right under my nose, back and forth in an arc across

the peaks of my philtrum. It comforted me, even when the satin fabric began to wear out and show its warp and weft.

That's how I am with my first sentences, with my mind instead of my lip, words instead of a satin binding, *this*, *this*, in a way that would be unsettling, were the gesture visible.

Thank God I'm invisible when I write, body and mind, entirely alone and wallowing at my desk.

6 | I DON'T THINK IT'S A BAD THING, TO WANT TO write a first sentence so idiosyncratic, so indelible, so entirely your own that it makes people sit up or reach for a pen or say to a beloved, "Listen to this." A first line needn't be ornate or long. It needn't grab you by the lapels and give you what for. A first line is only a demand for further attention, an invitation to the rest of the book. Whisper or bellow, a polite request or a monologue meant to repel interruption. I believe a first line should deliver some sort of pleasure by being beautiful or mysterious or funny or blunt or cryptic. Why would anyone start a novel, "It was June, and the sun was out," which could be the first line of any novel or story? It tells you nothing. It asks nothing of you.

Not everyone agrees with me, nor do all great novels have memorable first lines. Pull books from your shelf and you will find plenty that start with a month or day of the week plus the weather. Maybe there's a good argument: if you orient your reader on some level immediately, they will be ready for disorientation on others. Flatness can be a screen upon which brightness may be projected. Disorientation is one of the duties of fiction.

No, I insist. A generic first line is a failure of nerve.

7 | IT MIGHT BE HELPFUL TO BELIEVE IN ABSOLUTES when you're first writing fiction. *You can't have more than one point of view in a story. Novel chapters should be a uniform length. The present tense brings the reader in. The present tense is shallow as a dime. Epiphanies are how we understand life. Epiphanies are false, flimsy.* These absolutes should be as small and solid as training wheels; like training wheels, you can easily take them off later.

I have never encountered a rule for fiction I believed in, at least in the long run, apart from *Don't use a gothic font to make your work feel spooky.*

8 | WHAT DO YOU DO? *I'M A WRITER.* WHAT DO YOU write? *Short stories and novels.* Have you written anything I've ever read? *Statistically speaking, no.* What kind of novels? *Literary fiction.* What does that mean?

Nobody actually knows. Writing whose major aim is to be good, that aspires to be art no matter its content (though it can aspire for plenty of other things, too, including commercial success). Arguments about genre are pretty dull. When I was a child writer in the 1980s, literary writing was thought to be only a certain kind of realistic fiction, though there was evidence all around, stretching back to the origins of storytelling, that great literary art could involve miracles, monsters, love stories, the impossible yet true. I myself like art with magic and monsters, love stories, murders, and unhappy couples drinking whiskey; I like art that involves space and time travel and science, illustrated narratives; I like art above all, work that wants to move and surprise me, with lofty aims and a wish to be original. Of course I have my snobberies, but these involve uninspired prose and ineffable sadness.

I try not to dispense imperatives. All my advice contradicts itself.

9 | DON'T FOLLOW WRITING ADVICE LIKE A RECIPE. A cookbook's goal is to teach you how to create a soufflé that looks pretty much like other people's soufflés, which makes sense for soufflés. Note when a piece of advice strikes a gong in your soul. Note when you consider throwing a book across the room. Read fiction this way, too. What we love is inspiring, but what we hate is instructive. Hatred has edges sharp enough to use as a protractor, is magnetic enough to find true north.

Any writer's ideal craft manual must be bespoke, like a suit, made to measure. Write a manifesto aimed only at your own work without worrying whether it applies to or offends anybody else in the world. Address, in your silent heart, punctuation, plot, character, all your picayune concerns and grandiose plans, all the things that made you want to be a writer. Make it living, an armor-clad list that might change. It will be dearer to you than any other guide.

10 IF I CAN BE IMMODEST (I'M WRITING A BOOK; OF course I'm immodest), students over the years have suggested that I write a craft book. I've never been interested. No writer should ever approach a genre cynically. Many so-called literary writers decide to try their hands at a thriller to make their fortune, except they don't like thrillers, and they write bad ones, and they do not make their fortunes.

I don't like craft books. It's possible that I've never read one through. I distrust both rules and optimism, and the combination gives me the heebie-jeebies. *Craft* feels like regarding a vast tapestry and saying, *This is how I wove the blue part.*

When I write, my own decisions are guided by delusion, heartfelt wishes, hubris, and a fondness for running jokes, not clarity, structural integrity, or literary merit. We are not meant to know what we're doing. I'm not meant to know what I'm doing. Spiderwebs are sturdier, made as they are by engineers, but they're my inspiration, unadorned or jeweled with dew.

11 WHEN I WAS IN GRADUATE SCHOOL, I HAD CLASSmates who derided the thesaurus, who insisted that if you didn't know a word, if it didn't jump to mind, then it didn't belong in fiction. *Ten-dollar words*, they might say of vocabulary they didn't like.

I like all reference books—I have my grandfather's first-edition *Oxford English Dictionary* in thirteen enormous volumes, which I consult as often as the up-to-date *OED* online—but for inspiration and joy, there is nothing like a thesaurus. (I'm too fond of the word *joy*; I've looked it up in my Roget's and not found anything better. *Afflatus* was one of the related words offered under *joy*: *excitation*, an enticing word I guessed most people wouldn't know and which might suggest flatulence, with which it shares a root. I looked up *flatulence* next—*Looking Up Flatulence in Roget's Thesaurus* could be the title of my memoir—and found some wonderful words I might use elsewhere: *petillant*, *crepitation*.)

What joyless duds those people were in my grad program, who abstained from the thesaurus and tried to get everyone else to as well, members of the Iowa Linguistic Temperance Union. "You're drunk," they might say to me and my favorite writers. "Drunk on language." They even had tiny hatchets, the pens they used to cross out any words they deemed superfluous in somebody else's work.

12 THIS BOOK ISN'T ORGANIZED AS RIGOROUSLY AS A thesaurus. Its arrangement is what made sense to me—

vague broad concepts, digressions, flights of fancy. Organization is not one of my skills, but other people's organizational brilliance makes me swoon, like grace on the dance floor and polyglotism, and so a professional has created an index, though I have amended it.

This book is designed to be read through, but that's not a requirement. You may open it anywhere, skip around, or turn to the back to look up *metaphor* or *digression* or *Roget, Dr. Peter Mark*, who wrote in the introduction to the first edition of his thesaurus, "The communication of our thoughts by means of language, whether spoken or written, like every other object of mental exertion, constitutes a peculiar art, which, like other arts, cannot be acquired in any perfection but by long and continued practice." I am much of his opinion. He is one of only two other writers quoted in these pages.

13 | IF YOU READ THIS BOOK AND THINK, *THAT'S NOT what my teacher says*, and *That's not what my favorite craft book says*, I'm sure you're right. Writers disagree with one another, necessarily.

14 | ORDINARILY, I DON'T THINK OF A PARTICULAR audience when I write. Posterity, perhaps. But not *the reader* or *a reader* or any real-world friend, no matter how close.

This book is different. It has to be. It's meant to be of use. Art should be of use, too, of course; it has always been of use to me. In fact, I'd be desolate to think that my own books were not, once published, useful. But I don't think of usefulness when I write, what my words might mean to a stranger. I'm much more self-centered than that. I care what they mean to me.

Writing a craft book requires a different sort of self-centeredness. Self-importance, perhaps, my least favorite sort of egocentricity.

15 | IF YOU'RE WRITING A BOOK, I TELL MY STUDENTS, you better make it a book of your heart: something you suspect only you can write, something that will menace you if you don't get it down on the page. Too many people try to write somebody else's book, hoping that it's publishable.

I wasn't ever interested in writing a craft manual because I didn't know how to make it a book of my heart. But I grow older, and I know I won't teach forever, though teaching means more to me every year. I like thinking about fiction; I like talking to myself.

One of my students, a serious musician, suggested that (because I hate the word *craft*) I might prefer *technique*. Yes, much better. *Technique* is forward-looking, aimed at art; *craft* feels always like it's looking down at a bowl of something searching for shape. Maybe it's just that it's both verb and noun. It conjures in my mind sculpting with bad material, already drying out as I try to shape it. As a writer I do so little deliberately that I don't think I could explain to another person how I do it; as a teacher I don't believe that I can tell somebody the steps that will result in their own original work. Impossible! Nobody could.

Even so, I've taught creative writing for thirty-five years, longer than I've been publishing books, and I am now filled to the brim with opinions. "I don't think I'm right," I tell my students, "except I'm pretty sure I am." I believe in modes of thinking, not rules. At heart, as both fiction writer and teacher, I'm an aphorist and a metaphorist. Even when it comes to advice, I'm mostly interested in dispensing interesting and persuasive language. I hope to provoke my students into thinking the most interesting thoughts that they can, so they can teach themselves how to write.

16 | SOME OF MY STUDENTS HAVE GONE ON TO SUCcess, have written and published extraordinary work that has done well in the world. Pride in somebody else's accomplishments has always struck me as an odd emotion, vampiric and interfering. Still, of all the useful things teaching has given me—an ever-changing way to think about my own fiction, a sense that I know what younger people are preoccupied by, a livelihood that is never the same year to year, faith in my own life's work (my liveli-

hood is teaching; my life's work is writing)—the thing I take the most unattractive pleasure in is having read parts of brilliant books before anyone else, in class, during thesis work, or even before, in an application for grad school. No, I don't feel pride, but something darker: exclusivity, as close to being in with the In Crowd as I have ever been.

Sometimes I read a book by a young writer I have never met, have had nothing to do with, and enjoy it so much I look for my name in the acknowledgments.

17 | OCCASIONALLY A STUDENT WILL BEG ME FOR A rule. "Just one," the student will say. "Something, anything." I refuse.

18 | NO GOOD WRITING RESULTS FROM ASSIDUOUSLY following a set of rules. When a short story fails—when people read your work and are confounded—it's because the story is breaking rules it has set up for itself. Time moves in a way we haven't been taught to follow. Characters act inconsistently, or like clichés, following patterns of human behavior from outside the story: movies or television or bad fiction or received knowledge. The level of reality fluctuates for no reason. The story hasn't taught you how to read it.

If a good short story arises from following rules, it's despite, not because. That story might have been better, even great, had its author thrown away all outside rules.

This is true for novels as well, but people are less insistent that novels have rules, or perhaps they're worse at making them up.

Different writers need different advice. Different projects by the same writer, even. Nearly any piece of standard advice I've ever given out has over the years been shown its opposite by some brilliant book or another.

19 | HERE'S WHAT I'M LEFT WITH:

Ambition is everything. Fiction isn't ballet. It's not marathoning. You don't have to start small, with drills or exercises; there's nothing you need to perfect before moving on. Your budget for characters and sets and props and visual effects is infinite. You can splash out for equipment, but it isn't necessary. You should attempt everything. Ambition in fiction is merely the willingness to make mistakes. Mistakes are essential. It's not ice-skating. You won't break a bone. Sometimes a young writer decides to put off writing certain things, thinking they're too "technically difficult." This is a bad idea: if something excites you, don't wait. You might forget what interested you so, and, moreover, there are some things you can only write when you're young, and some things you can only write when you're old. You can always try to write the same thing when you're older; it will be a different book altogether. Like love itself, which is different at different times of life. Not less passionate or more impetuous, not deeper: the quality of the depth is different. Life changes you. It changes you on the cellular level. You learn astonishing things; you forget astonishing things, too, so completely that, looking back, it feels like a loss of faith. But you have only put your faith elsewhere. Your vision changes even if trained on the same thing. Some great writers produce nothing but the same book over and over, written at different ages, with only the occasional clunker.

Concentrate on process. When you're uncertain about the writing itself—the sentences or the content—write through it. If a page is impossible, try a sentence; if a sentence won't come, take notes. Writing is a form of thought. Any superannuated writer will tell you—I'm one—that years after the end of any writing class or program, it isn't the most promising writers who are still working, still publishing books, it's the most bullheaded. I'm one of those, too. Don't be afraid to romanticize your process, as long as by *romanticize* you mean *make lovable.* This only goes for good habits. If you romanticize your bad habits and deficiencies—a too-common thing for writers!—you will grow to love them, and you'll be perfectly happy never writing a thing.

Be stranger. Embrace your particular oddness. Don't give up your obsessions. They are dear to you: they are what make your work original. Be open to new fixations in life as well as writing. When you are fascinated with a subject or place or image, that fascination will exist for the fiction you write about it. Perhaps this seems obvious: of course you should be interested in what you write about! You might be surprised at how many otherwise excellent writers choose material almost at random, a sort of frame to arrange their sentences and characters upon. These writers would rather be good than interesting; they worry about being caught in a passion. But what the writer isn't interested in will never interest a reader. Your work may be beautifully formed, articulate, full of meaning, but if you're not interested in it, it won't have a soul.

20 | EVERYTHING I SAY IS TRUE ABOUT WRITING IS true for me. I understand it's not true for all writers. *Most* of the time I understand.

II

21 | YEARS AGO WHEN I WAS IN GRADUATE SCHOOL, my head was filled with rules for fiction, edicts from professors or classmates, a few foolish notions I came up with myself. These rules were based on the anxieties of the time and place, 1988–1990, the Iowa Writers' Workshop. Plenty of writing advice comes out of the anxieties of the time; in thirty years, at least some of today's common advice will seem old-timey and wrong.

We were told, or told ourselves, a lot of things. For instance, we should strive to be timeless. No very specific historical markers, nothing that could be seen as only now. In this way our work wouldn't become outdated. As though we could keep that from happening! I had classmates who said that fiction shouldn't be political, who intoned at every opportunity, *Show, don't tell*, or *Write what you know*, or *Kill your darlings*.

People said, *Show, don't tell*, so often it had the valence of a mob threat, something everyone knew you should do because the made guys said so. *Snitches get stitches.* I still don't know what it means exactly.

Write what you know. Subtext: maybe you don't know anything. Subtext: if your life hasn't been interesting, you can't be a writer.

Kill your darlings. If you love something, kill it. If it comes back to you, kill it again.

It's true that such pieces of advice prove the power of language, because they sound plausible even though they're devoid of meaning.

I can still picture the faces of the people who said these things to me (as some of my classmates can surely picture my face, saying something ignorant) because it was so long ago. My grudges are fossilized, preserved in excellent, unmalleable detail.

I loved graduate school: I made dear friends at Iowa who are still dear to me, whether or not we're still in touch. We took one another seriously. Nothing is better. That might be my number one piece of advice for young writers: find the hardest-working writers you know; take one another seriously.

22 | YOU SHOULD DISMISS GRUDGES WHEN YOU CAN. If they stick around despite everything, they probably mean something. Use them.

23 | POSSIBLY THE MOST UBIQUITOUS ADVICE IS THAT you must write every day. *Real writers write every day—*

that's what the director of the Iowa Writers' Workshop told us at our first-day picnic. Plenty of writers do. Make it a job. Sit at your desk and put your time in, first thing in the morning, four hours or five hundred words or five pages. Do the math: in a year you'll have a draft of a book, even if you move slowly.

It's excellent advice for those for whom it is good advice, and, I imagine, satisfying to dispense. Nothing ambiguous about it. I would go so far as to say that everyone should try daily writing. You might find it changes your life.

As advice, though, it's not universally useful. Not everyone can write every day; not every writer wants to or works best on such a schedule. I became a writer so I wouldn't have to do math or keep accounts. I can hear the voice of an every-day writer even now: If you wanted to—if you were *serious*! No: by circumstance or temperament, some writers can't or shouldn't. Many people work on timetables run by the needs of others: small children, elderly parents. Other people's illnesses; their own. Their own need to work a job to support themselves or others.

There are circumstantial reasons not to write every day, but you don't need one if writing every day makes you write badly. That's reason enough.

Worse: if you believe you must write every day and life intervenes and you stop, it can feel as though you've stopped for good. Too late to pick it up again. You might even feel ashamed. Writing becomes an unpaid bill. You can't even open the envelope. You stick it in a drawer so you don't have to look at it. Then the time away from writing stretches on.

24 | WRITING ISN'T BALLET, NOR PIANO. IT SCARCELY takes a single literal muscle. You won't injure yourself, writing after days or weeks of not writing; you won't have atrophied. Indeed, you may be a cicada of a writer, back full force after going away. You might be an annual, or a shook-up bottle of soda pop, more forceful when you resume.

If you've stopped writing for any reason at all, you can start again, from the exact place you left off or someplace even better. The reasons you stopped have changed you as a writer. Made you more interesting. In your time away, you haven't lost a step or a chop. You've probably gained some.

25 | LOTS OF PEOPLE SPEAK SCORNFULLY OF PEN-and-paper questions after literary readings, meaning generic mechanical questions: *Can you tell me about your process? Do you write by hand or on a computer? What time of day?* These are concrete questions about work instead of art: answerable, opposable. We writers believe that everyone else is doing it right while we bumble along in the gutter; we also believe that it's the rest of the world who bumbles and only we know the True Way.

Ask yourself those pen-and-paper questions, as though you are both audience member and visiting writer.

Or think of yourself as a science experiment. Try out everything to see if it works: early rising, late night, nice pens, crappy pens, the notes app on your phone, voice memos. Listen to white noise or music. Some of these experiments will only show what doesn't work. Make your space as amenable to work as possible. One year—one whole year of my life!—I wrote almost nothing because I lived alone in an apartment with plenty of room, a place I never had a single visitor, and I had crammed my desk in the corner of my bedroom next to a cast-iron radiator in such a way I had to clamber into the chair. This difficulty meant I almost never sat down at my desk to write. I certainly never sat down idly in my desk chair to read a book, an essential step in my process. When I moved house, away from the radiator, I immediately began writing. You might get away with moving the furniture.

26 | MAKE PROCESS (AND ONLY PROCESS) A CONTEST with your writing friends (and only your friends): how long you work, how hard. What weird complex note-taking system you have in place, the beauty and obsessiveness of your notebooks. Whiteboards, murder boards, charcuterie boards: whatever fuels the work. Trash-talk. Self-aggrandize. Challenge. I once told a friend that one day I worked so hard I scared myself, and I saw an answering

fear in his eyes—I scared him, too—and this is one of my favorite writing memories.

27 EVERY-DAY WRITERS HAVE A CLEAR ANSWER TO the question, *How will you get work done?* Me, I harness the power of my own self-loathing.

Self-loathing is a common commodity among writers. An uplifting craft book would tell you that you must forgive yourself before writing, that writing is *hard*, but I believe self-loathing has its uses, if you know how to angle it. Don't think of days, but weeks or months, a period of time in which you want to get work done. Say it's four months. You know that you have enough time in those four months to amass some pages, even if week to week you don't know where you will find those hours or minutes. Decide what you'd like to accomplish. Make it wildly ambitious, more than you think is reasonable.

Think: *How mad will I be if I don't get this done? How much will I hate myself?* Travel forward in time in your mind; make yourself really feel it. Put yourself into your body and take it on: the misery, the self-recrimination, the shame.

Travel back in time to the current moment. Realize that you can avoid these terrible feelings: all you have to do is work. Not every day. For you—for some people—the manageable units of time involved in daily writing aren't useful. Remember what you want to avoid: the nauseating feeling of having wasted a block of time.

A whole stretch of the calendar allows you to be more grandiose. If your aim is unreasonable, and you fall short, you won't feel too bad; if your aim is modest and you don't meet it, you will be crushed.

This method is the only way I get work done.

28 IN REMEMBERING MY TERRIBLE BROWN BLANket, I saw those warts and polyps, saw the matrix of threads in the satin binding as it wore out, even though I hadn't thought about that blanket in decades. When I didn't have the blanket to hand I could replace it with my own hair pulled across my lip like a mustache. I used to twirl my hair, too, and when I had a lock tight around a finger I liked to rub it with my thumbnail in a way that reminded me of the satin binding of the terrible blanket. To remember a childhood's sensory diversions and discomforts is the surest way to remember childhood, if that is the subject of your fiction. I had forgotten all of this until I remembered the blanket. Objects always conjure the past.

My writing habits are like that blanket, like a lock of hair snug against the second joint of my pointer finger. They comfort and anchor me and free my brain to think of other things.

29 WHEN I SPEAK AT WRITING PROGRAMS AND SAY with certainty that not every writer needs to write every

day, that I myself don't, without fail afterward one of the resident faculty will take me aside to say, "It's so interesting that you don't write every day! But I really think writers have to."

Their eyes are bright and panicked. They have issued this proclamation to their students. Real writers write every day. Why won't I just say so?

I don't believe it. I've never managed it. I haven't been great at making anything a job in my life, including my actual jobs. I always do too much or too little; I overvolunteer or I goldbrick. I've never been a person of moderation, though I have tried. Sometimes I write every day for months, but never with a sense of proportion. Is it a matter of psychology or neurology? *Laziness*, I used to think, and vowed continually to start my new life of discipline. *Tomorrow*, I told myself. *Monday, then. Okay, April.* I did try. When I was young and struggled to write interesting fiction every day, each morning was anxious, another day I might fail to buckle down.

And yet I persist in believing that I'm a real writer. I've never doubted that I am. My work, yes, I have doubted. My work ethic, and my reputation. Not my identity. I write; I am a writer. My qualifications are that I say so.

I understand that this can seem simultaneously glib and daunting. You might think it's a philosophical question. Am I a writer? A *real* writer, as the director of my graduate program specified long ago, scaring the bejesus out of all of us?

Am I a writer? is the sort of question (there are a lot of them) that seems deep but only wastes time. It's a binary question and—*To be or not to be* aside—no binary question is all that interesting, at least until it's answered.

If you call yourself a writer, whether you've written that day or month or year, you go into the world as a writer. Anything you see becomes more interesting because of your acquisitive writer's soul. A middle school production of *The Three Musketeers* in which the cast wears expensive rented capes and cheap store-bought plumed hats and their own dress pants and leggings, their own black sneakers and ballerina flats. The young lifeguard whose dark manicure has grown out, like waxing moons. A man in the grocery store who says into his phone, in a voice of love, "You're crazy. You're crazy. You're certifiably insane." A colleague, now buttoned-up and dull, who reminisces about her time as a teenage huffer of paint. You don't need to write any of this down. You could. You could have a little notebook; if you remember to carry it around, you're better than me. To consider yourself a writer as you move about the world is—I am a true believer—a beautiful way to live, a form of open-mindedness, even in terrible times. Here life is, going on all around. It is a form of writing itself; if you do it, you are a writer. It's likely to lead to putting words down on a page, at least a few, but even if it doesn't it can make you feel alive. Lucky. Luck you can make yourself.

So much of fiction is a trick of the mind. (Much of life, too, but my only expertise is in fiction.)

30 IN THE PAST FEW YEARS PEOPLE HAVE BECOME fond of the phrase *imposter syndrome*. "I suffer from imposter syndrome," a young writer might say, meaning they don't deserve what they've achieved, or, in its worst form, are afraid to dare to try. As though this isn't the human condition. Imposter syndrome sounds fantastic. It probably comes with a cape and a false nose and the ability to perform surgery without a medical license. What it means is: fear of failing. Calling it a syndrome instead of a feeling suggests that it can't be tampered with. It's not a problem to be solved, but something you will have forever.

It's not that I'm unsympathetic. No, clearly I am: I have just said that I have never doubted that I am a real writer, which is true. I have only doubted and loathed my writing and excoriated myself for not working harder.

Don't make a journey out of something that can be a decision. This is a corollary of *no binary question is interesting*. If you have received something—a place in a writing program, a compliment, an acceptance—do not wonder whether you deserve it. That is a question aimed at the past. You have it; the answer is yes. Turn your eyes to the future and put all your worry into your writing.

Am I good enough? is, on the other hand, an interesting question to write *about*. You could do worse than to take all your personal, worrisome flaws and put them into your characters. To feel ashamed about writing isn't interesting, but writing about shame is fascinating. A jealous writer may get no work done; a jealous character can scheme and murder and say astonishing things. You might even discover that once you have removed your flaws to use them in fiction—like a splinter, a bee's stinger—they no longer bother you.

III

31 MY FIRST POEM, WHICH I WROTE WHEN I WAS FIVE:

Owls are wise
And full of surprise.
They sleep all day
And work all night
Trying to scare
The robbers with fright.

I was a child who always wrote. My older brother was very good at drawing. It was much exclaimed over, how good he was at drawing, and he was also shy, so at family gatherings he drew instead of making conversation, leading to more exclamations. If this sounds like the bitter complaint of a snotty younger sister, it is. I wanted to show off but could not draw, nor sing, nor play an instrument. So I wrote. *I'll show them*, I thought.

I'll show them is an excellent reason to write. *I'll show them* is a solider jumping-off point than *I hope I'll prove myself*. It has sustained me for some time, with a variety of antecedents for *them*. There are always new *thems* to show.

32 IN 1990, JUST AFTER I TURNED TWENTY-FOUR, I started a fellowship residency that required nothing of me. I was given a small apartment in Provincetown, Massachusetts, and a minuscule monthly stipend. I had attended school since age four and had been employed since age fifteen. Now nobody expected me to do anything but write, and soon I put myself on a regular schedule.

I woke up and I planned to write. I cleaned my kitchen. I planned to write. I read a book. I planned to write, but by then it was lunchtime, and then I had to clean my kitchen again, and then it was probably time for a walk. In this way I procrastinated until eight p.m., when a paroxysm of self-loathing would propel me to my desk and I would actually begin. Then I could write for hours. Why didn't I just wake up and sit at my desk at nine a.m. like a functional human being? Why didn't I do something else with my days if I never got to work until evening? I tried both. Without the day's allotment of increasing self-loathing, I wrote badly. Dully. My characters talked about cake. They examined the tines of their forks. It took them paragraphs to cross a room. Somehow the process—focus on today's portion of work, one sentence after another—flavored the work itself. I plodded. The work plodded. Slow and steady may win the race, but it doesn't whip the wind through your hair.

33 IN THOSE DAYS, AN ALL-NIGHTER WAS LIKE AN ocean voyage: you only had what was around you and for a while you were between shores. The distraction of the

World Wide Web was a few years away, and outside of certain cities, there were few all-night establishments. Even television, if you had one, ended at some point. A waving flag would appear on the screen, the national anthem would play, and you would feel a strange existential unease: Something was over, but what? It couldn't just be the end of the broadcast day. In other words, I chased myself around my apartment until I exhausted myself and came to heel and wrote all night, alternating cans of Diet Coke and bottles of beer. Sometimes I smoked. I took up knitting to avoid smoking and produced a baby sweater with a checkerboard front that looked beautiful but upon examination had been produced by a maniac: the stitches were so tense it could have stood up by itself.

In those days I had more superstitions than a baseball player: I needed a certain chair and time of day, a window to my right. It was part of goading myself into the correct sort of frenzy.

I still need that chair, still prefer (though don't require) a right-hand window. Life goads me now, though possibly not often enough. Months go by when I don't write. When school's in session, I manage only notes and idle thoughts. My favorite part of teaching is reading student work. This means as I walk around in my own life, or swim, or drive, the books I'm thinking about are not my own.

I worked as a public librarian a while, forty hours a week; I wrote every evening and got plenty done, but soon enough I'd used up my generous vacation time—four weeks, thanks to my union—for writing-related travel, and so I quit. I squeaked by on my writing for a bit—fiction and freelance; I had a brief and awkward career as a celebrity profile writer—and then I worked as an itinerant visiting professor, teaching a single semester a year, leaving me most of the year to write. These days I live with other people, including another writer with an extraordinary work ethic whom I love entirely. (It's useful for lazy writers to throw in their lots with industrious ones.) At forty-four, I achieved respectability in the form of a job with tenure, which required that I teach both fall and spring. I should have adapted my work habits so I could work year-round, but somehow never did. So I romanticize the work habits I have.

I have two armchairs in my campus office, one of which belonged to my grandfather McCracken, where I sit, one nice sturdy blue chair from university surplus for visitors. I've been told that my office is like a therapist's. People cry in the blue chair (about both life and art) or outline their plans for novels, or ask advice, or just gab. I'm available for all of it.

Once my semester is over, I turn my grandfather's old chair, in which I have sat and read and written for thirty-four years now, away from the blue chair, where my students sit, so that I can look out the window. It is a grave, delightful ritual. I recently told some students about this, and they gasped, were wounded at the thought that I wanted to look away from the place they occupy. That is exactly my aim. I want to be kind enough that they expect me to be looking their way; I want to be mean enough to enjoy their hurt when I look elsewhere.

I do enjoy it, I'm afraid. During school breaks and leaves, I am a different person. I read nothing in progress. I meet no students. I do write every day, not because I've planned to, but because it's what I must do: I've done the math. I know what I need to accomplish to stave off self-loathing.

34 IN GRADUATE SCHOOL, I SENT OUT MY FIRST stories to literary magazines, as I had been instructed: you put your manuscript into a manila envelope alongside another manila envelope—the next size down if you cared about such things, the same size folded in half if you didn't. The second envelope was self-addressed, with enough postage attached so the magazine could return your story with a rejection note. In those days, you could only get bad news once a day, via the US mail, and I walked home from class with my eye trained on the mailbox on my front porch, one of those wall-mounted numbers with a flap that opened at the top like an envelope itself. If I could see a stripe of manila, my story had come back, hopefully in good enough shape to mail to the next place. No matter what sort of rejection it was—form, or with a handwritten note—I would burn it in the barbecue in my backyard. I had a friend who papered her bathroom door with hers; when it comes to writing, nearly any ritual will do.

Good news could come through the phone, but only during business hours. When my first book was on submission with a publisher, I stared at my black rotary phone and said my agent's name aloud in a pleading, incantatory way.

(The rotary phone was an affectation in 1990, the equivalent of carrying a flip phone now, which I also do.) A few years later, I got an answering machine with two miniature cassette tapes, one for my outgoing message and one for incoming calls, a high-tech object that, when I called from an outside line, answered after one ring if I had a message (then I would punch in a code and hear it), and four rings if I didn't (so I could hang up and retrieve my coin from the pay phone). Long before all telephone messages came to your pocket, before most civilians had electronic mail, I was so obsessed with my answering machine that I called it from every pay phone I passed.

As long as I can remember I've been distracted by the romance of communication, the possibility that somebody might phone to declare their love, or send me an envelope with an unexpected check *and* a declaration of love. The mail truck, the UPS truck, the flower delivery van: they could all be bringing riches of some kind. When the mail arrives, no matter where I am, I wonder if there's something for me. The mere presence of pigeonholes anywhere makes my heart flutter, though my logical mind knows that my name is not taped above or below any of them.

Courting disappointment, hoping for the best. This, too, is training for writing fiction.

35

I HAVE LOVED THE INTERNET SINCE I WAS A LIBRARY science student in 1992 and had to write a user manual for my program's resource center. (Long ago, the internet was something that needed a user manual.) I love it, it's a menace to me, the whole burbling noise of it running underneath everything, audible unless I take extreme measures. I block it on my laptop, using an app; I don't carry a smartphone. I take these precautions not because I'm pure but because I'm not.

This isn't a problem of the modern age. I seem to remember that Victor Hugo went to his room and stripped down and had his friends, or manservant, take his clothes away, so that he couldn't do anything but write.

It's all right to use prosthetic self-discipline. It's easy to despise those people who just know how to work, who don't procrastinate, who feel neither the terror of the desk nor the rising joy of playing hooky. But it makes no difference whether you work hard and easily or must trick yourself into it, as long as you work.

36 INSTINCTIVELY I BELIEVE THAT NOBODY CAN write well unless locked in a distractionless cell of their own making, because I cannot. Logically I know this isn't true. Some of my students regularly get together to write at coffee shops and bars. They set timers for silent work sessions; when the alarm sounds, they're allowed to chat until the next work session begins. Friends who cannot hold still or shut up are discouraged from coming back. To write in company is a way to be held accountable. You're visibly writing. If you stop, you'll be visibly not writing. It works for a lot of people.

Not me: I'm an animal who can't abide being seen as she eats. I am distracted by proximity and noise—though only noise caused by nearby humans. Sirens, gangs of kids a block away, thunderstorms, no problem, but one summer when I was working in my campus office, somebody outside my door unwrapped a sandwich loudly, slowly, *sensuously*, and I nearly barged into the corridor to complain.

37 WE ARE ALL DOGS. WHAT WORKS FOR AN AUSTRALIAN shepherd would kill a corgi. A greyhound needs different discipline than a clumber spaniel, though they both have work to do. You have to figure out what will make you heel, sit, stay, be it other people or running out the clock on the day's distraction.

38 I WORK IN ISOLATION; I MAKE MY OWN EFFORTS visible to myself. I don't do this consciously. It feels akin to nest-building. Not a bird's nest: a rodent's, or marsupial's, or wasp's. I make a physical mess all around my desk, built of notebooks, notepads, postcards, books, binder clips, butcher paper. The books are in piles, some stacked open, spines up like roofs and some spread out across the carpet like a carpet. If I'm really stuck on a sentence I will turn to my IBM Selectric typewriter. Hum, smack: I can track my progress down the page, type the sentence over with the minorest adjustments, ask myself like an optometrist: *This* or *this*? I can rip the paper from the platen with its haptic

stuttering roll and crumple up the page and throw it over my shoulder. More refuse for the nest. More evidence that I'm working.

I don't aim for a word count, but early in a project I attach big pieces of paper to the shelves and at the end of the day write down how many words I've written. In the morning, I vow to meet or exceed it.

39 NO WRITING IS WASTED. EVEN WHAT WE THROW out is progress. The problem with computers is that most of us erase unsatisfactory sentences as we compose, and so there's no record of all the fumbling we do in a day. The delete key disappears our words letter by letter. The feeling goes into our very psyche. Nothing remains, not so much as a ghost of an accomplishment.

I don't *really* start at the beginning. By the time I sit down to write, I have taken notes. Nothing extensive or organized. I will have filled the first six pages of a dozen notebooks of varying quality: the finest Italian leather with handmade paper; cunning waterproof notebooks that fit in my hand, with paper made (claims the cover) of stone; Moleskines when I'm taking myself seriously; spiral-bound notebooks from the CVS. At one book festival I looked for a something upon which I could scrawl the brilliant thoughts occasioned by a poetry reading, and ended up at a 7-Eleven, which stocked a bizarre 7-Eleven-brand journal. In that aesthetic nightmare of a notebook I never got past the first page. I still own it, though. Then there are the receipts, napkins, and envelopes because, despite owning a library of notebooks, I often don't have one to hand. I wrote some of this book on a flayed Pepto-Bismol box, the only thing I had in my purse at a jazz show that, like the poetry reading, gave me thoughts I found interesting. I still buy notebooks when I am moved to, because I know that some thoughts are ephemeral and yet valuable. They're made of the moment but deserve to outlive the moment, like certain postcards sent from a person you love.

Through some neurological quirk I am able to address an envelope in penmanship of some beauty, but I cannot read 47 percent of what I write down in notebooks. *Slow down*, I tell myself. *Pretend it's an envelope. You are writing this down because you want to remember it. Don't call yourself names, even accidentally. You are doing your best.*

40 | OF COURSE I'M JEALOUS OF THE WRITERS WHO monogamously wield expensive pens, who have on their shelves a series of journals with uniform bindings, each filled with expressive, or at least legible, handwriting. The diarists, with the stick-to-itiveness to write every day, if only a line or two. Those people with sufficient self-interest, -knowledge, and -discipline, no fear of seeing themselves on the page, no fear of being boring . . .

I'm jealous of everything except what they write, and so I console myself: despite four decades of resolutions and notebook purchases, of telling myself that this time will be different, this year or semester, this particular volume—

look at the red leather, the ribbon bookmark with its little notched end!—after everything, I don't think I've ever filled more than a third of a notebook. I've certainly never finished a diary, or even made it out of January. I must conclude that it's part of my process. All of it: the wasted money, the hopeful scribbling, the time spent wondering what I meant by *potato family resemblance* or *lofty*, the lines I remember writing down somewhere but can't find: it all goes into the writing, somehow.

I believe in resolutions, not just about paraphernalia but the whole enterprise. *This book will be different*, I think of every book. This novel will be the one I write in one or two drafts. This will be the short story where I understand the characters from the start, the short story collection where I won't repeat myself accidentally, where I will achieve my particular goal: a universe made of smaller universes. No duds. No story that people like better than the others. I'll apply myself. I will not watch bad television, won't read anything but great literature.

When it comes to fiction writing, there are some lessons we must never learn.

41

IN HIGH SCHOOL I WORE LURID, ODDBALL clothing. Even by the standards of the early 1980s, historic in its gaudiness, I stood out. Once in a hotel in downtown Boston, where some friends and I had crashed a science fiction convention, an older boy said to me, in the voice of a friendly entomologist, "You dress like this all the time, don't you?" He was a senior at my school, he explained. I didn't know him. I remember what I was wearing, or perhaps I've filled it in: a pair of garish plaid parachute pants, mostly purple and hot pink, tight at the ankles; a black turtleneck; a knit double-breasted vest that picked up the minor line of marigold in the plaid. A vintage hat, perhaps. Converse All-Stars in purple or silver lamé. Nothing the least bit sexy or revealing: allure was never the point of my getups.

How did it make me feel, that this boy I'd never met recognized me because of my clothing? Did I feel *seen*?

No: famous.

Vintage dinner jackets, mother-of-the bride dresses, home-tie-dyed painter pants. I chose my clothes because I was a girl and chubby and socially awkward, full of shame and arrogance. The easiest way to hide a thing you're ashamed of and love is in plain sight. Lamé, plaid, lace, literal camouflage, DayGlo. You hope people don't notice you at the heart of all that blare. You hope they do and love you extra.

That's exactly why I write fiction.

IV

42 THE FIRST INKLINGS OF A PIECE CAN ARRIVE IN nearly any form: an image, a line of dialogue, a line of narrative, a setting (place or time period), an abstract idea (*I have always wanted to write about a scientist who is a devout believer in God*), a title, a plot, a structure, a character. A character might arrive in any way: as a predicament, or a mustache; as a role (for instance a mother or a priest); as a physical fact. Concrete or abstract, it doesn't matter. Myself, I know the height and weight of my characters before I know their names or secrets.

43 SOME WRITERS COMPOSE DRAFTS QUICKLY, carelessly. They don't worry about beauty at first, or music. They know ahead of time that they will write many drafts, and the most important thing is to get the shape of the thing on the page. In order to begin, they tell themselves it's all right to write badly. Otherwise they might never get out of the first paragraph. They don't look back till it's time to revise.

Other writers must be painstaking from the start. Every morning, they reread what they've done so far and edit sentence by sentence. They cannot go forward until the thing feels right.

I am, in my way, a painstaking drafter: I sit down, read the entire book from the beginning before I go on, print it out an environmentally irresponsible number of times and scribble all over it. Still, there's nothing exacting in my process. Nothing tidy. I don't produce nearly-there drafts, even when I tell myself that I am. But I can't bear to write what strike me as bad sentences. In the innermost chamber of my writer's heart, the only thing I really care about is language, and I cannot think about fiction except in sentences. Sentences are how I lower myself into the dreamworld, how I know my characters (body and soul); sentences are my bucket and my torch.

44 SOME PEOPLE WAIT TO START A NOVEL UNTIL they feel confident enough, but you have to be a little panicked to make it across the ocean in a rowboat.

45 PROPONENTS OF OUTLINING, LIKE EVERY-DAY writers, like to recommend the process to everyone. They are talking to themselves, announcing how their own brains work. As for me, I have tried outlining before I start a project, and it looks like this:

I. The Waxmans arrive in Iowa.
   A. Family unhappiness.

1. The loss of furniture.
   i. That buffet, a wedding gift, was an act of revenge.
      a) List of Great-Grandmother Waxman's grudges.

. . . until the outline threatens to slant around the back of the page.

There's a wonderful moment while writing a book when, after swimming alone in the ocean of your dreamworld, you can sense it becoming actual, you can imagine how another person might navigate it by the landmarks you have installed, but you don't want to arrive at that shore too soon. For some people, outlining is a form of thought: free from sentences and paragraphs, they can make meaningful decisions about their books. The outline prolongs the dream. Others of us dream in sentences only. We dream as we draft. Nothing is possible (I am talking to myself) without language. I figure things out. I write with the abandon of a tourist. What interests me at first might bore me later. That's all right.

No process is wrong that leads to a first draft of a book.

46 | ONE OF THE REASONS I'M GRATEFUL FOR YEARS of teaching: I have thought so much about plot and character and narrative choices in a nontheoretical way, about setting and structure and time; I have learned to see how essential every aspect of fiction is—to other people's

work—that I'm forced to accept that my own books can't be merely collections of sentences that I find aesthetically pleasing. For young writers, *I'm not good at plot* generally means *I don't really care about plot*, and so it was for me, but now I care about plot. I couldn't do without it. It is still the last thing I know about anything I write.

47 SOME WRITERS KNOW EVERYTHING ABOUT THE world of a story, setting and plot and characters, chronology and conflict, before making a single narrative decision about who's telling the story and how. Who's telling it and how: that's all a narrator is, and for some people that comes late in the process. Before they write a word, they can see a character move around their settings; they wonder, but do not know, whose angle on events will be most complicated, compelling—one character, or three, or all of them—and in what proportions. These writers can hold huge amounts of information in their heads. They make narrative choices deliberately.

Others might be unaware they're making decisions. A first line appears in a particular voice: already the story has a first-person narrator, is in the past tense, is a retrospective voice telling a story that happened years ago. It's worth thinking about the effects of different narrative decisions, and worth remembering that no decision is permanent. Soldiers at attention and choir members on their risers are reminded never to lock their knees, because if they do, and they faint, they will go down hard.

48 | FICTION ISN'T CHEMISTRY, AND NEITHER IS NARRATIVE. When we speak of narrators we might think of three kinds: first person, second person, third. *I*, *you*, *they*, but within each category there's measureless variety. My mother, a sometime English instructor, taught out of a book called *First Person Singular*, and I remember how mysterious and enticing the phrase was. I instinctively wanted to be a first person singular. I still find it enticing. Once a published writer said to me that he didn't like first-person narrators because you always had to decide the literal circumstances of the narrator: Was it a written diary? A jailhouse confession? A monologue? If monologue, delivered where and how, and who was listening? From what exact distance was the narrator talking? How did we readers have access to this telling?

He said this as though this was a scientific fact: no first-person narrative could exist without specific explanation.

I was flummoxed. After a moment I asked, "How do we have access to characters' heads in third person?"

His voice was bewildered as he said, "I never thought of that," but I believe he believes that his point still stands.

49 | BEWARE OF ANY DISPENSER OF WRITING ADVICE who deems one sort of narrator better than another. Such advice is astonishingly narrow-minded. We are neurologically different: not all people perceive a first person the same way. You can use second person within third; third

person within first. I've never written anything entirely in second person, but I love it as a technique, lapsing into it for passages where I want to accost or unnerve the reader. You might, too.

50 | YOU MIGHT USE FIRST PERSON SINGULAR, FIRST person plural, second person, and third person in a single paragraph. (See above.)

51 | ALL NARRATORS ARE AGREED-UPON MAGIC, first, second, third. Fiction gives us the ability to know strangers, multiple and singular, from the inside and the outside, to feel the vibrating border between out and in. That is its particular power above all other forms. It doesn't matter how it accomplishes this. A first-person book *can* present itself as a written narrative, but it may also be that we are privy to a character's internal monologue, things that are thought but that could never be spoken aloud or set down on the page. Only fiction allows this sort of sustained intimacy.

52 | ANY FIRST PARAGRAPH WILL LOSE YOU SOME readers, those who flinch at first person or prefer fiction in the past tense, who may think, *I have never been interested in novels set before the Enlightenment*; or, *That particular name for grandmother gets on my nerves.* It's fine to lose read-

ers. When a writer is compelled by an aspect of narrative—the second person, shifting tenses, fragments—it suffuses the work, can win over readers, though some readers will remain unwinnable. No fiction is universal, thank God. Nothing is blander than universality.

53 | FIRST-PERSON NARRATORS ARE MOTIVATED TO tell their stories. They want to explain or convince, to answer the first question of fiction, which is also the first question of the Passover seder: *Why is this night different from all other nights?* First-person narrators know the answer in a way that characters in a third-person narrative don't. A first-person narrator might not know *why* they're telling the story, but they know they are; they know that they must keep their audience interested. First-person narrators can think of themselves as the center of the story (and universe) or as peripheral players. They understand some things, and not others; they try to make sense of events either for themselves or readers, and in this way even the most malign, difficult character, in narrating their own story, can be very dear. What is a human life other than the process of trying to answer, *What just happened; what does it mean?*

54 | FIRST-PERSON NARRATORS MAY PERSUADE OR prevaricate. They take readers into their confidence. They may flat-out lie. A first-person narrator who regularly lies

or clearly doesn't understand the truth of the story they tell is generally thought of as an *unreliable* narrator, though all narrators are unreliable in their own way on the scale of reliability that also applies to human beings. Unreliability can arise out of naiveté or deviousness, but only works when it's part of the narrator's way of thinking, created from within. I despise an "unreliable" narrator who has been put together by their maker from the outside, who believes patently unbelievable things, and whose lies are instantly visible, whose unreliability is like starch in a voice, serving only to stiffen.

Take a look at this schmuck! such writers seem to say of their narrator. *Can you believe him?*

55

A FIRST-PERSON NARRATOR IS A KIND OF BATHYsphere, a one-person submarine, an exploratory device lowered into the fictional world. You don't want to spend too much time wondering how it works while it's actually moving through the water. *Train yourself to think like the narrator* may sound like vague advice, but, like a lot of writing, it's not a process but a mode of thought. Try to feel the character come over you; try to feel yourself in their body. Understand them so well that you never wonder, *What do they do now?* You have made this character up: you know.

If you aren't thinking like your narrator, you will find yourself stalled at a series of forks in the road—*Do I go this way or that way? Does she go this way or that? What would she do in this situation?*—and then you have lost momentum. Forks in the road can seem earth-shattering, but they are, in the end, binary questions. Best to keep going.

56 | YEARS AGO I HEARD A STUDENT ASK A WRITER, "How do you know when you've chosen the right scene to write?" *What a good question*, I thought. (When some writers say, *What a good question*, they mean, *I have thought a lot about this very topic myself.* I mean, *I have no idea; I wonder, too.*)

The writer answered, "I figure it's like life. You make a decision and you stick with it. You go forward."

As both life and writing advice, this astonished me, an inveterate ditherer. Who would I be without my regrets? What am I supposed to do with my hands if not wring them? I've grown to understand this answer, at least as writing advice. It's more important to choose an interesting event in fiction than a meaningful one; that is, it's easier to make something interesting and strange meaningful than it is to take a feeling of abstract import and try to guess what event might illustrate that in an interesting way.

Moreover, as a writer, in fiction you might as well run counter to your own human habits. You might as well be decisive if given to dithering. Might as well be ruthless if you're milquetoast, or tender and expressive if you're repressed. All-knowing when in real life people stymie you; benevolent; unafraid of parties and confrontation. At the very least, it's good practice for the rest of your life.

57 YOU MIGHT GET TO KNOW YOUR FIRST-PERSON narrator by writing a great deal of biography (in your head or notebook or separate computer file). List the character's settings: home, childhood home, work, favorite restaurant, places of recreation. List the people the character encounters in those places, and what your character thinks of them. You can research in more literal ways—reading books about their vocations and avocations and geography; watching movies; interviewing people who have things in common—but a great deal of research, that is, gathering information outside of composition itself, can be done through mere thought and note-taking.

None of this is essential. The way you get to know your characters doesn't matter, but if you get stuck, amassing details that don't seem germane to the plot can help. Not all characters want to be known; the most complicated ones may fight against it. Even the most reliable narrator will try to hide something, and characters are always standing in the way of other characters. Whoever your narrator is, they want the attention and love of your reader. It can be hard to see around them, or into them. Out-of-the-text writing—in a journal or a new file, in the notes app of your phone or on a piece of drawing paper—is a way to get a new angle. Changing the physical way you get words on the page can help you think differently.

58 ALL MY EARLY FICTION, AND FOR YEARS, WAS written in first person. The only way I could understand

characters was by listening to them; I crawled inside their heads and looked out. When it didn't work, I felt like a bad puppeteer; when it did, like a method actor. I was inside, not up above; I pretended to be somebody else until I was that person. This was how I wrote my first two novels and quite a few short stories, resulting in one or two main characters and many minor characters; I somehow couldn't understand multiple characters from the inside. Not that there's anything wrong with minor characters. I love them: brightly colored, capable of wit, unbeholden to the great emotional machinery of the work at large. But my minor characters had no life in my mind off the page. They didn't trouble me. These days I want characters who trouble me, and I try to think of all characters as major, even if they appear only briefly in a book.

I still use first person as a tool when I don't understand a character, though in my fiction I now favor third-person narration. I write some pages—in one of my partially filled notebooks, or on my thrumming IBM—in that character's voice. By the end of the first sentence I understand them better. Then it deepens.

59 | BE CAREFUL OF TOO MANY INDIRECT CONSTRUCtions in first-person narratives. *I saw*, *I realized*, *I thought*, *I knew*. These are sometimes called *filtering verbs*. On a grammatical level, the construction weakens verbs: the subject of the sentence is *I*; the main action of the sentence is reduced to an object. For instance:

> When I walked into the kitchen, I saw that my mother was opening a canned ham, the sort shaped like a church window, with a curvilinear peak and a flat bottom. I could see her forearm shake with every turn of the little key that undid the belt around the can's perimeter. I knew she would cut the ham into large rectangles and then small rectangles so she could fry it, and I remembered she told me that her own mother had cooked ham for her this way, and that she hated it, though now she claimed to love it. I knew she felt the same way about her mother. Yes, I thought: first hate, then love. In my head I heard my mother say it: that was the right order for a happy life.

Nothing that the mother does in this passage is direct action; all action is seeing, remembering, thinking, knowing.

> In the kitchen, my mother was opening a canned ham, the sort shaped like a church window, with a curvilinear peak and a flat bottom. Her forearm shook with every turn of the metal key that undid the belt around the can's perimeter. When the ham was free she would cut it into large rectangles, and then smaller rectangles to fry it. Her own mother had cooked ham this way, and my mother had hated it but now loved it. She felt the same way about her mother: first hate, then love. That was the right order for a happy life.

It's not that an indirect construction is never necessary, even at length, but verbs are descriptive language as sure as adverbs and adjectives, and anything that continually weakens or attenuates them weakens everything else. Moreover, when you write in the first person, you want your narrator to be a character with other characters, not held back at the remove of description. You don't want them forever in their heads. You want them in the room, on the ground, obeying the same laws of physics as the other characters. Indirect constructions keep narrators narrating, instead of acting and interacting. We know, in a first-person narrative, that if there is an unascribed thought, it is the narrator who thinks it; a visual description, it is the narrator who sees it.

60 | LOWER THE BATHYSPHERE INTO THE OCEAN SO you can describe the ocean, not solely the inside of the bathysphere and its pilot.

61 | MOST OF THE GRAMMAR I KNOW I LEARNED from my tenth-grade English teacher, Mrs. Hubbard, whom I loved. She taught us how to diagram sentences. I'm not sure whether children are taught to diagram sentences anymore; I think it's one those things of which people ask, "When will I use this in the real world?"

Use? What a terrible thing to ask. The real question,

for any subject that is taught, is *Will I think of this again? Will it haunt me?*

As it happens, I think about diagramming sentences, *and* I use the knowledge in a professional capacity. I think about solving algebraic equations, Latin, the dissection of fetal sharks, the Fertile Crescent, the poetry of Phillis Wheatley, and the assassination of William McKinley. At least once a month I think of the *Hindenburg*, its galumphing beauty, its ten round trips between Germany and New Jersey before it famously ignited. I think about how the flames scoured away the outside to show its metal frame, the people who died, and the dozens who survived—all of this in my head because in fourth grade I wrote an essay about the *Hindenburg*, assigned by an otherwise incompetent teacher who once slapped me on the back as I was erasing something, which is why I have a piece of graphite visible above my eye nearly half a century later. Inoculated by pencil, I later became a fiction writer.

62 IF YOU ARE ALIVE IN IT, THEN IT *IS* THE REAL world. I am speaking of both school and fiction.

63 A FIRST-PERSON PLURAL NARRATOR–A TOWN that speaks as a whole, or a team of hockey players, or all the children of a family—is a form of magical realism, with all the power, thrill, and strangeness. Beautiful and weird,

to swim in a collective consciousness, to turn attention with others (like a school of fish) to another character. A simultaneity of perception! Most fiction is concerned with what characters make of other characters one at a time. First-person plural gets at how much conjecture is involved when human beings try to understand other human beings; it allows us to gaze at characters in both company and privacy, moviegoers staring up at a star on a screen.

It can also feel in its way shallow, as though we can't get deep into our narrators and they themselves can only guess at the complexities of those they describe. This isn't necessarily a problem. Different creatures live in the shallows than in the depths, as deserving of our regard, as fascinating, too.

64 THERE ARE MANY KINDS OF SECOND-PERSON narrator, among them:

In which the *you* is a sort of avatar of the reader: *You walk down the street and wonder how your life got this way.*

In which the second person is a fully developed character with biography and personality separate from the reader: *Your name is Isobel Herbert, you are twenty-seven years old, and you can feel the pavement through the hole in your shoe.*

In which there is a first person addressing a specific second person: *By now you've arrived in London, you're setting up your stall in the Spitalfields antique market, and I am trying to picture your table as you arrange the little perfume bottles, the silver spoons your grandmother collected so you do, too.*

A story of instruction, written in the imperative: *Straighten your back in your theater seat. You paid money like anyone else. Do not apologize for your height or the width of your shoulders or any other quirk of your body.*

A good second person is uncanny and complicatedly bossy. You're told to do things, or you're told you're already doing things. The narrator is issuing commands but is also in your head, instructive, dislocated.

Second-person narrators can free a writer from the constraints of first or third: you don't need to think about why a character is telling a story. In some ways you're asking the reader to supply character motivation. This can also be a drawback: some readers dislike being told what they're doing. *You walk into a bar—*

I do no such thing. I gave up drinking a decade ago.

65 | THIRD-PERSON NARRATORS HAVE MORE FAMILIAR technical words attached to them—third person limited, third person omniscient, third person objective. These words all have to do with how close the narrator is to the characters and how many characters' minds the narrator can access. The terms sound scientific, as though there are understandable rules or conventions, mechanical or chemical, but a good third person is closer to God than to science.

66 LIKE GOD, A THIRD-PERSON NARRATOR IS A GASeous invertebrate. It isn't a person, reliable or unreliable. It doesn't *know* things: it has access. Like any gaseous substance, it can permeate certain membranes and not others, can move through space and time and points of view in a way no mortal being can.

Closer to God—or at least third-person narrators have god-level powers, privy to the thoughts of crowds and single lonely people and dogs and the dying and dead and taxidermy bears. Not all third-person narrators take advantage of these powers, as not all gods interfere in the lives of humans.

67 SOME THIRD-PERSON NARRATORS ARE SO CLOSE there's no place between the narrative and the thoughts of a character; some narrators are at a slight distance, still close, but with a sense that the character's thoughts are being described by the narrator, not simultaneously conveyed. Some are outside entirely. A fluid third-person narrator might assume all of these distances and points between in a single work of fiction.

With third-person narrators you can write deeply about characters who wouldn't tell their own stories, or can't, who have no interest or lack the language. Children, for instance. Ordinary children can make dull first-person narrators, because they are, as human beings, every bit as interesting and complex as grown-ups, but with lagging vocabulary: their feeling and fears and ambitions and fantasies and philosophies are beyond the words they have to describe them. With third person, you can get at the intricacies. Most really good first-person child narrators are prodigies of one kind or another.

If you want to write about children, try to remember what it felt like to be a child. Children are people on the face of the earth, and if they enter your work you must remember that. They are not symbolic (of innocence, or cruelty). They are sense-driven beings who put their hands all over everything, and, like any human beings, should not be used as objects. Relatively few of them actually lisp, and if they do it is not notable enough to render phonetically.

(Phonetic dialogue should be used sparingly. Paradoxically, phonetic spelling moves words away from the audible into the visual: you see the word, inspect the letters, and only then have some sense of sound. Much better to use vocabulary and sentence structure to get at accents or any idiosyncratic way of speaking.)

68 | IF YOU DON'T KNOW HOW TALL A FIVE-YEAR-OLD is, do not guess and say their head comes up to a hip or a doorknob.

69 | IF YOU ARE IN A WRITING CLASS OR GROUP YOUR fellow writers will insist there are rules governing third person with multiple points of view. I don't know why this

is, just that somebody will explain in a weary voice, like a mechanic who understands carburetors. Don't listen to them. As usual, the only rule is that it has to work: you have to take your readers with you, so that their energy isn't used up in wondering whose head they are in. You want your readers to marvel at the inconsistencies of the human mind, to know more than the characters themselves do. This is one of the pleasures of reading, and speaks to every level of *craft*, or whatever we're calling it: how a reader can see the plot unfold while characters are at the mercy of it; can know that one character thinks his marriage is happy while his spouse knows it isn't; can see the pattern of the book's structure while characters are entirely unaware. No character ever knows that a literal chapter in their life is about to come to an end, but readers can, and it's heart-breaking.

70 IN FICTION THERE ARE NEEDFUL MYSTERIES AND needless mysteries. If the author and characters know a secret and only the reader is left in the dark, that's a needless mystery. If you withhold a fact and think, *When I reveal this, it's going to blow the reader's mind*, nine times out of ten it will only make them think you've been playing cards with an ace up your sleeve. If you trick your readers, in other words, by hiding a pertinent fact, they won't think you're good at writing. At best, they'll think you're good at tricks. Fiction can disorient readers, but if they don't know where they are, if a piece of fiction continually shuts

a reader out of what's happening, who's talking, what year it is, then they will feel as though they're on the other side of the door of an interesting party. Some personality types enjoy this feeling of exclusion. Not many.

Altogether it's easy to overestimate the pleasure readers take in figuring out facts, who is speaking, their relationships to one another, where they are, what time period or geographical location we're in, what level of reality. It's not that everything must be instantly clear, only that if everything is obscure, readers are only looking down at their feet, wondering where they are, not up at the glories of your fictional universe.

Needful mysteries are about the mysteries of life. What can be done and not done, what can be seen and not seen. Needful mysteries tend to be mysteries to the characters as well.

71

I HAVE STUDENTS—BRILLIANT STUDENTS—WHO struggle with exposition. Perhaps in their youth somebody influential barked, *Show, don't tell.* Perhaps some of their influences are cinematic—very sensible; one's literary influences should never be only literary—and in movies characters don't explain what they pass as they walk down the street, or tell you about their inner lives. There are exceptions, of course, as there are in any art: art can't exist without exceptions, and (unlike science) those exceptions never, ever prove the rule.

But cameras *do* offer exposition continually. The actors themselves do. The camera lets you know that a character is walking down Sunset Boulevard in the early 1970s; the actors let you know they're mostly delighted to be in each other's company, but the one guy, the shortest guy in the squarest clothing, he has reservations: you can see them on his face. I mention the time period because that's the sort of thing I beg students to just *say*, without hokiness or making it a puzzle: no looking at a newspaper or describing bell-bottoms or a character saying, "As you know, the US *did* put a man on the moon a few years back." Fiction is made of words. It's *good* to tell you readers things. That act of telling can free a reader's attention up so they can interpret instead of decoding.

Some third-person narrators switch points of view on a timetable: at chapter or section breaks. Point of view is treated like a cafeteria tray with compartments; one character's thoughts never spill into the next.

Other multiple-POV third persons switch within chapters, occasionally even within a paragraph:

> Caroline had asked her tenants to water the plants on the terrace, and they had agreed, and she knew they were not doing it. She asked her ex-husband, who still lived on the street, to go by, hold his camera up over the fence to take pictures, and he agreed: he didn't still love Caroline, not really, but her devotion to her plants was endearing

> and troubling—the sort of love she'd had for the horses, when they lived in the country; she felt she understood them more than she did people—and he took the pictures as a kind of alimony, and as a way to keep thinking of her. The tenants—visitors from the north—also thought of her every evening as they watered the plants and watched them die nevertheless. They knew nothing of plants, or horses, were only just managing to keep each other alive. All they knew was that they were paying rent, and even so, they had a tenant, Caroline, who would blame them for their shortcomings. *I hate her*, thought the tenant wife, even as she—like Caroline's ex-husband, like anyone who'd ever met Caroline—wanted to please her, too.

This might seem tricky until you get the hang of it. You have to make sure you're not dancing while looking at your feet, overly aware—as with those old-timey instructions for dance that use footprints on floor mats to tell you where to next step—that you must put your foot *here* (count one, two, three) and now there (one, two, cha-cha-cha). I used to think that a multiple third-person narrator was beyond me, that my brain couldn't do it or that I wasn't interested: I was drawn to the inner workings of singular characters, in first person or close third. Then my brain shifted or I taught myself how to do it, and now I can't do without it.

If you had told me when I was twenty-four that I would favor the third person, I would have sneered at your condescension; I would have believed you understood nothing. Indeed it is condescending to tell any young person what they'll be in the future; the future will tell them soon enough. Not all writers improve, but they should change. I don't think third person is better than first, it's just what I've done for a while. Lately I've heard the first person whispering in my ear again. I'm not changing my mind. I'm just interested in something else. A different kind of character; a different kind of book.

72 | FICTION IS NOT THE CHA-CHA. IT IS A FLUID SUBstance; remember its fluidity, even if you only sometimes take advantage of it.

73 | NOT A RULE BUT A GUIDELINE: IN A THIRD-person narrative that has access to multiple points of view within a chapter or section, switch points of view to give us information we can't get otherwise, through the character you're already in or dialogue or even exposition. The new point of view should give some interesting new tension; it should pull at the previous point of view.

If you switch points of view all the time, whenever a new character talks or moves, it can be like skipping a stone over the surface of a lake: the stone will travel a great distance without ever getting deep.

Or: if you switch points of view all the time, it can be like an animatronic display, the band at Chuck E. Cheese or the Hall of Presidents at Disney World, where a single figure lights up and moves in slow motion and the other characters are motionless in the dark while the illuminated character delivers a speech.

74 MY GRANDMOTHER TOOK ME TO DISNEY WORLD when I was seven. I was too lily-livered to keep my eyes open in the Haunted Mansion, but sat in the little car and buried my head in my grandmother's armpit while she laughed and said, "It's funny, it's funny." The other rides I think of all the time, each one a kind of narrative—20,000 Leagues Under the Sea, Mr. Toad's Wild Ride—you are in danger except you're safe, or safe except in danger, and now it's over.

No, that's not right. It's a Small World has no narrative, only a theme, which is why it's such a famous nightmare, and why I remember thinking—wide-eyed this time, but still terrified; it's not funny, not funny!—that it would never end.

75 THE PRESENT TENSE IN FICTION HAS BEEN around a long time. It's often beautiful, introducing dreaminess and doubt, or immediacy and propulsion. Fiction in the past tense has occurred; fiction in the present tense is ongoing. A first-person narrative in the past tense means that the narrator has (probably) lived to tell the story, and third-person past tense can have the weight of history: the

action is over and all that remains is relating it so we can understand what it means. The future of a past-tense narrative is the narrative itself.

A present-tense narrator feels more uncertain, or does to me, the characters at the mercy of time and the story unfolding in front of us. The future of the present tense is unknown to the characters, even a narrator, and so readers can feel very close to them. Real life occurs in the present tense; you are reading a book in the present tense about characters living in the present tense; everyone's in the same chronological boat.

76 | DID I SAY THAT REAL LIFE OCCURS IN THE PRESent tense? I don't believe that. We live in a great simultaneity. Sometimes you pay attention only to the thing in front of you, but generally you bring along your past—your obsessions and wounds and grudges—and your future—your worries and dreams. When you meet somebody you think you might come to love: that is a cacophony of timelines. When you visit a patient in the hospital, all the hospital visits of your life gather around your shoulders, like cherubs in a painting.

77 | NO, I DON'T THINK THAT THE PRESENT TENSE IS so different from the past tense. You, sitting there reading this book (or driving and listening, or standing and scrolling)—you have a past and a future as surely as you

did a month ago while reading a different book. In good present-tense fiction, memory and possibility pass their shadows over the characters no matter what. Without that, the present tense is a stretch of road through the desert in a cartoon, the odd cactus passing behind a car. The road itself is exactly the same. The car is the same. Even the cactus is the same: the car jumps in place, and the cactus moves across, goes out the wings, hurries back and makes its mark, reappearing as though it's a different cactus until it's left behind again.

78 SOME WRITERS ARE PARTICULARLY DRAWN TO the present tense, just as some are drawn to the third person or to the second. These affinities can change at any time in a writing life. The way we write is tied to how we process information about the world, is what I think. My early stories were in the first person because other human beings seemed unfathomable to me, but I believed I could understand a single person, what they thought, who they knew, what they made of their lives. My interest in nearly everything was backward, into history: it wouldn't have occurred to me to write fiction in the present tense. Then I flew a novel into the side of a mountain after years of work and multiple drafts. This was my second unpublished book. It was dead, but I was alive, and I pulled a story—present tense, though the novel was in past—from the still-smoking wreckage. The first story I'd written in years: I'd decided I'd never been a short story writer really;

I had always been a novelist, given to digressions, obsessed with the past.

That story is different from anything else I've ever written. There's future tense at the end, and second-person passages; multiple points of view; a ghost. I felt freer writing it than anything else in my life. I was alive! I could do anything! I wasn't a novelist, after all, but a short story writer! Later, I would fall back into my old patterns, though I am always trying to nudge myself into a similar state of panic and liberation, particularly when it comes to short stories: I have come to grief. I have survived. Now I can do anything.

79 | I WROTE THAT STORY TO STOP FEELING wretched. I've always found this wonderful motivation.

80 | YOU CAN GET AWAY WITH A LOT OF STRANGENESS at the end of a short story, in the last page or two. It's a kind of human flight. Take your readers with you: tuck them under your arm as Superman does with Lois Lane or Jimmy Olsen, show them things you cannot get to any other way, thrill them.

81 | THE SUBJECT OF MOST NOVELS IS TIME, IN A WAY. A short story can be brief enough that you don't think about duration, but time passes in a novel: it passes on

the page and it passes in the experience of the reader, an awesome thing to contemplate. That may be the reason so many first drafts of novels make time needlessly complicated, out of chronological order merely for suspense or for the writer's convenience and not because the book is interested in time or memory (both good reasons for writing a book out of chronological order). A secret is withheld, an irresistible but dense-as-fudge chunk of backstory is introduced, events take place over decades for no reason. It's subconscious, I think, an attempt to give the book some of the feel of life on earth, which, despite being technically in chronological order (or so most people think), is also always knotted up, with intimations of every epoch that ever existed.

If you compress time—not the book itself, just the period of time it covers, three months instead of three years, one week instead of three months—a curious thing may happen. Too much time, and it's like going into a room in a museum where paintings are hung at a distance from one another. The works are separate, connected by century or region or movement or only the viewer's attention. Move them closer, so they are hung in a group, and suddenly they affect one another, talk, pick up colors, gestures, angles.

82 | ONCE I HAD A WRITING TEACHER WHO SAID, *NO flashbacks*. No moving back in time at all. This was common advice for short stories back in the 1980s: time was supposed to go only in one direction, forward, and stories

were meant to be written mostly in scene. This teacher was interested in "realistic fiction." I thought I was, too; I believed I was writing it, though nobody agreed with me.

Time only goes in one direction, a flashback-hater might say, *and fiction should be a mirror of life.*

To repeat myself: time does *not* go in one direction, and while I, too, believe that fiction should be a mirror of life, sometimes it's a fun-house mirror and sometimes a house of mirrors, sometimes a two-way mirror in an interrogation room, the ominous shapes of surveillance more visible through the glass as time passes, sometimes it's a mottled mirror with half the silvering fallen off, or a polished piece of metal, or a shop window filled with mirrors so you can see passing forms in multiple iterations from multiple angles as well as in the plate glass itself. A convex mirror that blows you up big or shrinks you down to nothing, depending on where you stand. A cell phone with a filter or a video with a three-second delay. A side-of-the road mirror that shows around-the-bend oncoming traffic. A rearview mirror. A newspaper called the *Daily Mirror.* A mirror on a medicine cabinet as it swings open and tosses your reflection against the bathroom wall. A three-way mirror in a dressing room that reveals your whole self from unflattering angles. A mirror in a powder compact that shows only one feature at a time and can be used to spy on people across the room, if wielded correctly. A mirror on the floor playing a pond in a theatrical production. An actual pond, at twilight or noon. A camera obscura, a camera lucida.

Every mirror has its uses. The mirror in the corner of an elevator won't show the rot in your molars; the periscope won't reveal what's right in front of you. All mirrors are ways of confronting your mortality.

As long as it shows us something of the human, it doesn't matter. Even fiction with no humans in it shows us something of the human: the desire to escape being one; the terror, too.

83 | PERHAPS I CONTRADICT MYSELF. WHAT I MEAN: time in a novel should be fluid, not tectonic. Sometimes you need to move back or forward. Reading books that are out of chronological order for good reasons can be thrilling.

The ability to move a reader back and forth through time is one of the supernatural powers of a novel. Don't use it accidentally.

84 | SHIFTS IN TIME DON'T WORK IF THE MAIN STORY-line, the present time of the story (whether told in present or past tense), is treated as the *real* story, and a flashback merely a deviation from that. Flashbacks that are only informational—*hold on a minute, here's what you need to know*—are dead at the heart. A lot of exciting first chapters in novels are followed by mind-numbing second chapters that stop the book to insert seemingly necessary information.

Don't explain what triggers a flashback. Don't have a character shake their head to dismiss the memory upon the return. At the very least it's hokey, like an old-time sitcom when someone is hit on the head with a coconut and the screen goes wavy and we hear zither music, and we're back in time or in a dream and then, dream over, we return to the present, more zither music, more wavy lines. At worst it's a weak structure: the past time is *depending* on the present, attached at one spot. Picture it physically and you can see the flashback pulling down the timeline with its weight, returning to the exact spot it left. But if you move confidently away, knowing that the past runs alongside your story, and confidently back—then you can go wherever you want.

85 | PICTURE TWO PARALLEL RIVERS. WHEN YOU step back you will never be in the same place: something will have happened in the past to change the present.

Time is a river: it necessarily moves objects upon it. You can use it to deliver things, if you pay attention.

Time is a structure, particularly in novels: how it moves gives shape to the book, whether it's back and forth between chapters, or within them, or between parts, or straight ahead, a load-bearing beam. A flashback that departs and arrives at the same station in a book is a weak structure. It bears no weight. It holds nothing up or together.

86 | PRESENT TENSE IS EASIER TO WRITE THAN PAST tense, but an *interesting* present tense is much harder.

87 BEWARE OF ANY NARRATIVE CHOICE THAT YOU make because it forecloses possibility. You might do this subconsciously, because it solves certain problems; I do it all the time. Sometimes writers choose the present tense as a way to don temporal blinders, as though past and future therefore don't exist. A good present tense is about texture, not time, and should be as rich and complicated and full of possibility as the past tense. All narrative decisions are more interesting when you think about the mobility they grant you instead of the mobility they restrict.

Write in the present tense for the tension it provides, the sense that life can be careless. Choose a single setting because a house can be full of peril (memory, literal ghosts, plumbing) and not so that you can ignore the outside, with all its people and weather. Put two people at the center of your book because they will work each other over, not let each other off the hook. Choose a time frame because it's part of the great simultaneity, but remember all the other possibilities and time frames that exist. They're there, to regret, to offer relief. Know that you can mention the future in the past. References to other times can be a structure in your work, can bring in light, windows in an otherwise solid wall.

V

88 ONCE, AT AN EXCELLENT WEEKEND WRITERS' conference, I gave a craft talk. It was called *On Failure* and at least partly concerned why I refused to participate in karaoke. In the car from the airport to the conference site, one of my fellow writers had asked me what my go-to karaoke song was. I didn't have one. Everyone else in the car—two fellow faculty and the conference's organizer—seemed shocked. I tried to explain my own limitations—I don't like people and I don't like fun and I don't like being the physical center of attention, or playing pretend, or ordinary competition—but the truth was more complicated.

I am in my late fifties. Most of the odd mental habits of my teenage years are behind me. I no longer think that an article of clothing might change my life. I don't believe that I can transform my bad habits over the course of a summer in such a way as to cause my enemies pain. I don't memorize long poems under the delusion that someday I will be at a party where the ability to recite much of "The Ballad of Reading Gaol" will come in handy. But when I hear a song I love, late at night or driving alone, I sing along, con brio, pretending that I'm in front of a small adoring crowd, just as I did when I was fourteen, that much yearning and delusion.

There are plenty of talents I'd like to have: painting, acting, close-up magic. I'd like to tap-dance. To dance in general. To draw. To lecture off the top of my head. But I'm fine not doing any of these things. Perhaps I even believe I could, if I applied myself; perhaps one day I'll take lessons. I'll be a diligent student. I will practice, as I never did the flute. Would I trade writing for sculpture or grace on the dance floor? Of course not.

Would I trade it for the ability to sing really well in front of people? I'm not talking about a career as a vocalist, just the ability to floor a local audience, a room full of astounded listeners, a song in which I specifically command people to love me and they do. (The subtext of all my writing is *love me.*)

Treat me like a fool, treat me mean and cruel . . .

We didn't know she could do this, my dream audience thinks. *We didn't understand.*

But I can't trade, can't sing, and so I write on.

To generalize: most fiction writers wish they were really vocalists, and some fiction writers love karaoke because it allows them to live out their dreams. I save that longing for my fiction. I edit by reading aloud; I imagine myself in a packed theater, houselights down, no specific face in the audience visible. Man, do I knock 'em dead.

89 I READ MY WORK ALOUD FOR A NUMBER OF REASONS, only some of which have to do with vanity. When I write, I hear language, but it's not direct. Sonic, but not phonetic, a kind of burble that I find beautiful. Like swimming while nearby a band plays loud music: I sense the sound, and it's part of the experience, but not the entirety. Notes, not nuances. When I read aloud, I hear everything: accidental rhymes and repetitions, sentences that don't make sense, five sentences in a row that sound alike, inconsistencies and unparallel constructions. Using my literal voice puts me back in the work as opposed to above it, as happens when I read in my head. If I realize that I've stopped reading aloud, it's because my mouth knows the work is not so good: unclear, listless, unworthy of being declaimed. I read aloud to show off, but to myself. I'd be horrified if anyone could hear me.

90 WHEN I WAS IN GRADUATE SCHOOL, THERE WAS A lot of talk about voice. Not the voice that any one particular story or novel was written in, but *voice*, that thing that distinguished one writer from another. My classmates spoke of it as though it were a religious vocation, as though we were waiting for God to whisper in our ears: *This is it. Verily, you are a writer.* "I'm still trying to find my voice," people would say, ashamed, humble, self-important.

I think that's what they meant. At any rate, they had reduced complicated questions—*How do I write prose in my own key, in my own way? How do I make both beauty and meaning palpable to a reader? What sort of language sings to me, makes its own sense and beauty to me?*—and they have turned them into a single question, a note passed in junior high school math class: *do I have a voice circle one Y/N.*

91 YOUR VOICE IS MERELY THE IDIOSYNCRATIC LINGUISTIC habits, good and bad, that give you pleasure. Your own little indulgences, the way you form your thoughts, whether you like to repeat words or let your sentences go long or are careless, inconsistent with your commas. Voice comes from writing with an open ear and open mind. It rises up from the page. It doesn't descend from the ether.

Some teachers might want to make your personal language conform to Good Style. Don't let them.

All language needs rigor to avoid sloppiness, slackness, dullness, sentences that sound much better than they mean. (The unkindest thing I ever write on student manuscripts, and I write it often, is *Sounds good. Means?*) If you are a stylist, if you build your sentences in particular ways for good reason and take great pleasure in doing so, don't let anyone break your style. Break, as one breaks horses, to train them. (I think. I know nothing about horses.) You will need to understand your own style and come up with your own rigor. You don't want your habits to become affectations or automatic, things you do because you do them, devoid of meaning or surprise. Still, personal style may mean something to you as it does for singers and painters, saxophonists and illustrators—any artist, in fact. We admire a singer's phrasing and range, a painter's brushstrokes and palette. Prose should be no different.

92 ONE OF THE KARAOKE-PERFORMING WRITERS AT the conference—she owned a karaoke machine, so she'd given it some thought—told me that karaoke is about confronting your mortal self. (Karaoke is a kind of mirror.) What I think she meant: you put yourself in peril and you push through doubt and survive. The centerpiece of my craft talk on failure was my one experience attempting karaoke, during which I did think I might die. It took place in Provincetown, Massachusetts, a place I have made important, improving mistakes. I'd gone to Drag Queen Karaoke at the Governor Bradford, not intending, never intending, to perform, when I decided to sing a truly awful, retrograde, sexist song: "A Hundred Pounds of Clay." It's about God creating "a woman and a-lots of lovin for a man." Perhaps you've never heard of this song. Nobody at Drag Queen Karaoke had, nor anyone years later at the craft talk.

Even now I don't know why I decided to sing it, other than it was on the menu of available songs and I recognized it from the oldies station. Perhaps I though the oddity of the choice would mask my inability to carry a tune.

In other words, I had no connection to my material, and I hated my narrator, and I hadn't considered whether my audience would have any interest at all.

I know exactly nothing about music, but "A Hundred Pounds of Clay" wasn't in my range, no matter how you define *range*. I made it one line in, or three. If I recall correctly, the drag queens did nothing to stop me from bailing. Some failures aren't worth watching, even by those in the business of mockery.

What I discovered singing three lines of karaoke was that I didn't have the stomach for failing at it. To do anything, and enjoy it and improve, you have to have the stomach—the heart—for failure. *This is painful. I'm awful at it. A flop. Better not quit.*

93 I PREFER *FAILURE* TO *DOUBT*. DOUBT'S A WAVERing thing, never solid underfoot. It's tough to launch from the bog of doubt. Failure is hard, motivating. Those kinetic swings between delusions of grandeur and extreme self-loathing are how I get anything at all done. If you suffer from these extremes, they will afflict you all your life. At least, they have me: I require the momentum, which means I must accept sometimes that I've absolutely failed. Otherwise, I'm in the quivering zone of uncertainty, where I might be okay and might not. Quivering is movement without progress.

94 "A HUNDRED POUNDS OF CLAY" WAS THE LAST time I sang in public. The time before that was in the

eighth grade, when I decided to try out for the school production of *Oliver!* My best friend had a piano, and we flipped through her family sheet music and discussed what we might choose for our auditions, in the way that we readied ourselves together for school dances, curling and feathering our hair and wondering what we might dance to. I was aware that my friend was more musical than me, though like most thirteen-year-olds I still had one foot in fairyland; I thought it was possible that I had a beautiful singing voice that I'd managed to keep secret from everyone, myself included, like a birthmark that proved I was royalty.

I have always been given to fits of honesty over things about to become self-evident. In Paris, I declare, *Je ne parle Français trés bien*. At the *Oliver!* audition, I stood in front of the assembled music teachers and said, "I can't really sing."

The song that I'd chosen, which I had practiced alone and in front of my friend, was "The Theme from *M*A*S*H*." Perhaps you didn't know that "The Theme from *M*A*S*H*" has lyrics. It grieves me to report that it does. Not only is it a challenging piece of music, covering octaves and key changes, but its actual title is "Suicide is Painless."

It was this that I had decided to belt out in front of my junior high school music teachers, hoping to land the part of a plucky orphan.

"Congratulations," the nicest of them said when I had finished. "Most kids don't know they can't sing. You do!"

95 WHAT'S THE MORAL OF THIS STORY? FOR YEARS I took the congratulations to heart. *Know thyself.* I never again tried out for anything musical.

Now I think it's a story about ambition and longing. What I didn't tell those teachers, or my friend: I was obsessed with *Oliver!* When I felt misunderstood by my family I would go into the book-lined spare room we grandly called The Library, which also housed the hi-fi and the convertible sofa upholstered in an ugly, durable fabric called Herculon, and I would put on our copy of the cast album. I knew every word of every song. I was particularly devoted to "Where Is Love?," the eponymous Oliver demanding: *Love me.* I would sit under a table and mouth the words with passion and hand gestures.

The *where* of "Where Is Love?" is five syllables long, and I knew better than to sing that for the teachers, but I might have managed a painless "Consider Yourself." Painless for both me and the teachers. Instead, I chose an unrelated song, because I dreaded the judgment of grown-ups, not about my voice, but my longing. I didn't want them to know how much I cared.

96 I HAVE WRITTEN A LOT OF BAD FICTION IN MY time, not wanting to reveal my own longing to the world. I have worried about what I'm good at in writing and what I'm bad at, and every second of that worry has been wasted.

97 | THE MOST DIFFICULT THING FOR AMBITIOUS writers is to dismiss thoughts of what other people think. It's a paradox. You write because you want people to read what you've written and swoon or weep or even fling the book across the room. At the same time, you cannot care. Fiction writers are particularly liable to be control freaks, will want to manage reader interpretations. This is the reason for 97 percent of misused adverbs.

You have to write the best work you can and cede all interpretive control. Readers will think what they want, goddammit, God love them.

Why do I write these days? I want to be loved. But I don't care whether anybody approves of me.

98 | AS A TEACHER I WORK HARD NEVER TO OFFER approval or disapproval. Both are disastrous for a writer. A student will ask, for instance, "OK, what if I write a whole section from the sister's point of view five years in the future?" I answer, "Could be great! Could be terrible! Only one way to find out."

It's very human to want approval for your ideas. If you were a good student in school, you will have to work harder not to seek a stamp of approval. We slackers and class-skippers, we who had potential we never lived up to, we have the advantage here. Even writers who think of themselves as provocateurs write with disapproval in mind, itself a kind of stamp: easy to procure, a millimeter thick, a moment to apply. Approval and disapproval are very low ambitions.

Write for love and revenge, to change your life and the lives of others.

99 | VOICE, NO: NO NEED TO WORRY ABOUT VOICE. It's material that's the real question, the thing you must look for and dream about.

VI

100 SOME YEARS AGO, WHEN I HAD FOR THE FIRST time returned to the Iowa Writers' Workshop as a visiting teacher, a colleague (who'd also been my classmate) said he had a question for me. He wondered how I told my students what they should be writing about.

"I don't!" I said, shocked, as though he'd suggested an intimacy I'd never entertained. No, I told my friend, none of my business. Up to the writer. I will stick to my usual pedagogy, which is built on withering looks and illegible marginalia.

I have come to understand what my friend was asking. Every year, I read hundreds of applications for MFA programs (I teach in two). I judge contests and fellowships. What am I looking for? My answer used to be dull and incomplete: *The best writing.*

What did I mean by this? There's no such thing. We all want to believe that when we send our own work in for judgment, to a program or a magazine or a publisher, that our work will pass through some mysterious machine with an ultraviolet light which will reveal on our first page the inarguable word *literature*. But literature, created by humans, is likewise judged by humans, and there's a randomness to anything that has to do with art, dependent on a reader's taste, night's sleep, mood, prescription. Even more than that: Is this the third story that takes place on an imaginary island, or the first? Are all the stories accepted so far also in present tense? Does the reader insist he cannot abide fiction in which a dog dies?

Nowadays I try not to look for anything, to read in a state of innocence. (This is my preference for all art.) An application should not succeed or fail based on my expectations or wishes or preferences. I try to dismiss them. Of course there's work other people love whose charms escape me: fiction with its sense of humor amputated; anything with extreme gore unleavened by humanity; I struggle with elves, though not with ogres. Mostly I try to put myself to the side and look at the work.

Wonderfully and disappointingly, there are a lot of fine writers in the world. People whose sentences are beautiful (linguistic beauty, like physical, takes many forms, can come from spare clarity or antic sound or startling metaphor). There are writers whose characters from major to minor have pulses and souls. Writers of plots that pull you to the depths. Innovative writers who put together a story like nobody else.

What makes a difference to me as a reader is a writer's relationship with material.

I'm not *looking* for this, largely because it cannot be seen. It isn't technical. But, having been asked, I realize it's what I respond to. The writer finds the world of their fiction palpably meaningful. This is another word for *interesting*.

101 MATERIAL SHOULD BE PERSONAL IN THAT YOU should be personally interested in it: puzzled, intrigued, troubled. You should want to get to the bottom of it. Material needn't be something lived through, though it can be. *Lucky*, some writers think, hearing of another writer's eventful or terrible childhood. A complicated childhood full of privation and catastrophe isn't an inheritance that sets up a writer for life. It isn't even the childhood itself that's useful: it's that the writer is interested in the childhood and doesn't entirely understand it and works to get it onto the page, out of the body, so it can be looked at. Plenty of excellent writers have awful childhoods that they're not interested in and never write about; some do only later in life, when youth can be viewed through the telescope of time. This is true of geography, too: it can be easier to write about home when you've left it far behind. Then you can hold it in your palm, like a snow globe, and look at it from multiple angles without being overwhelmed.

102 SOME WRITERS ARE BRILLIANT AT WRITING about childhood. Others of us remember only dross and outrage. I have told you about my blanket. I also remember with great vividness sitting on a low stool in my Portland,

Oregon, living room and peering into a bowl of canned spaghetti that my mother had cut into pieces with the side of a fork, without my permission, as though I were a *baby*. This was the great passion of my preschool years. Later, in fourth grade, I was made to copy dictionary pages as a punishment for talking—there were two teachers, a mean woman who palpably hated children and a bungling man; the man often stole parts of our snacks, saying, "Here comes the popcorn monster!" (This is the teacher who accidentally pushed me into a pencil.) Eventually they left teaching and married and opened a high-end antique store on Cape Cod; I sometimes dream of bursting in and shrieking, *You taught me nothing!*

Outrage and dross. Early on, I would have said that my work—my short stories, because I was only a short story writer then—was emotionally autobiographical and factually fictional. Now my short stories are the opposite, events taken from my own life, picturesque but not meaningful, given to a character and made essential, transforming, defining. Those events aren't material; they are furniture that I drape material on. I'm much more cold-blooded as a writer now that I'm middle-aged, cold-blooded to myself most of all. Youth, middle age, old age—amazing that youth lasts the longest.

103 ANOTHER PERSON—A STRANGER SITTING IN THE next airplane seat, an irrepressible aunt, a parent—finds out you're a writer. Says, "I have a great idea for a novel.

Guaranteed bestseller. I'll tell it to you, and you'll write it, and we'll split the profits."

These enthusiastic aspiring collaborators! No mere idea is worth half the profits of anything. In the reality show of my fancy, I'd offer 5 percent, tops, for a really good idea. If it's not your material, you have to work hard to find out what interests you.

104 | YOU DON'T NEED TO WRITE WHAT YOU (ALready) know, because with research and hard work and pure will and a willingness to blunder and bomb as you write, you can make yourself know a great deal.

Write about what you know. If you already know it—if there's no mystery—what's the point in writing it?

105 | MATERIAL CAN BE—SHOULD BE—BOTH PERSONAL and abstract. Burlesque dancers of the early '60s; the difficulty of having a female body in the early '60s; canning salmon in Alaska; what it means to be working class among people who aren't; the intricacies of growing up in a family of eleven children; how familial duty can dog you all your days. Saginaw, Michigan, in the nineteenth century. The family history and the shame at the center of it. The lives of doormen. Competitive Ping-Pong. Forestry. Anything that lights up your limbic system will do. Even those things that no longer, you think, mean much to you, but once did: they meant everything.

106 | PEOPLE LOVE TO READ ABOUT WORK. ANY JOB you've had is excellent material for fiction—dishwashing, the law, cab driving, nannying, medicine, selling charity door-to-door. Moreover, if you can write with expertise about something, your readers will trust your expertise about the world at large.

107 | THE HIGHEST FORM OF INTEREST IS NECESSITY: the thing you must write. Necessity may grab you by the throat all the time or only now and then. It may frighten you. It often frightens me. *You have to write this*, necessity whispers, and you think, *Rather not*.

Then you do, and find it's the thing people respond to, because a feeling of necessity is one of those emotions that, occurring in the writer, transmits to the reader.

Necessity can arise out of joy and love, but it usually involves a wish to understand something you don't. You write to fix something on the page without killing it, a vivarium built of words.

Or it may be that a catastrophe has befallen you or your characters. You know you have to write about it, but you don't want to. Still, there necessity is, beating its wings at the back of your head. Obey it. Chances are writing about the difficulty will be easier than thinking about it, in the way that the shadows things cast are often more terrifying than the things themselves.

For me, writing about horrible experiences or thoughts is a way to get them out of my head, out of my body, stow them in a neat box I can move away from me. Anything I have written about, even the worst things, I can talk about easily. It's what I haven't written about that renders me speechless.

108 EVERY WRITER KNOWS THE WORRY OF WONDERING whether anybody would be interested in the work. Like imagining all other people's negative reactions to your work, it's pointless.

Your own interest is what's important. Your own interest matters, cannot be faked, is the animating spirit. God-level stuff.

109 WRITING *IS* WEIGHTLIFTING. LIFTING A SMALL weight, no matter how often or at what speed, will not train you to lift a bigger weight. (Bigger in ambition, not word count.) To get stronger, you must always lift a weight that's a little uncomfortable. In this way, you damage your muscle fiber, and it knits back together, and you can lift ever heavier weights.

110 TERRIBLE THINGS NEED NOT HAPPEN TO YOU, IN order to be a writer. Terrible things *will* happen to you, if you are a human. You needn't write about these things on purpose. You will probably write about them eventually, one way or the other.

111 *A WRITER IS SOMEONE UPON WHOM NOTHING is lost*: come, ye emotional magpies, use it.

112 ANOTHER PARADOX. WRITERS SHOULD PUT meaning into their work, but not point it out. What concerns you—sexuality, rural life, black humor as a form of God's love, precarity, work, trauma—will be in anything you write. Plants do not make oxygen on purpose. They can't help it. It's a by-product of their existence. Meaning—even the notion that life is meaningless—is a by-product of ours. It's the reader's job to find it. Do not explain to readers that something simple is quite remarkable: show readers the simple thing so they can see it is.

113 I STILL DON'T TELL STUDENTS WHAT THEY should write about. My grandfather Jacobson's favorite cousin, my first cousin, twice removed, Elizabeth, once told me about following a car manual to fix her REO, step-by-step. She took apart the engine one instruction at a time until she got to the line, *You are now in the master cylinder.* She thought, *What am I doing in the master cylinder? I don't belong here.* So she followed the steps in reverse and put the engine back together.

I never want to be in the master cylinder of somebody else's work, though I do want to help my students get to the master cylinder on their own. I would never tell another writer that they should write more directly about some aspect of their life, that they should change the sort of fiction that they're interested in. The only jobs a writer has are the ones they take on themselves.

(I do sometimes say, having heard a good anecdote, "You should write a story about that!")

114 | IN MY EARLY STORIES, AN OCCASIONAL NARRAtor in a short story resembled me: a little petri dish with a few cells scraped out from under my fingernail, never developing into anything much, a child among eccentric grown-ups who knew the major story was not her own. I didn't know anything about these characters, hadn't bothered to try. Did I lack self-awareness, and so made my fictional counterparts unknowable? No, I was unspeakably vivid to myself, full of humiliation and desire that I gave to other characters—a maiden aunt, an elderly murderer, a middle-aged widower. Like leaving underpants in other people's laundry hampers: I wanted to get caught.

115 | WHAT IF YOU WANT TO WRITE AUTOBIOGRAPHICAL fiction featuring characters based on real people? Disguise them. Don't disguise them. Worry about their feelings; don't. Leave them out entirely. Know that there is not a right answer, and that once you change specific details that seemed inalterable you will discover that it's not a big deal.

Some people will recognize themselves in places they aren't. Some will not recognize a photorealistic portrait.

116 IF YOU CHOOSE TO KNIT YOUR FICTION OUT OF your own autobiography, you will never run out of material. Same for things imagined. Material, even the most personal, is a self-refreshing resource.

Autobiographical work is not superior to imagined, nor vice versa. Writers are given to proclamations on the subject, depending on what they themselves write at the moment.

117 PLENTY OF WRITERS SPEAK OF THEIR CHARACTERS as though they're separate, living humans. She took over the book; he refused to be silent; it's as though I'm simply channeling my characters: I sit down and let them talk. Channeling, as a medium does at a séance—as a medium claims to do. *I love her*, these writers say of their characters, which is not immodest because, after all, who they are praising is not themselves.

No, says the practical writer. *The characters are made up. They feel real to you because I am good at my job.*

No channeling here. I believe in nothing supernatural (despite being superstitious); I don't believe that there is a story whizzing around the world that lands upon me at the right time. I do not traffic with the ether. There's nothing at all cosmic about me, including my work.

On the other hand, it feels as though there might be.

Something about my neurology causes the sensation: science can explain how I write, even if I can't. Moments, even hours, of inspiration, when I understand things all at once that determined thought cannot uncover. My best work happens at a subconscious level; I discover what my characters want and where they are going simultaneous to the writing itself. My decisions are not conscious, even if I acknowledge that I must be the entity making them.

When I revise I see all sorts of patterns. A character who is mentioned in passing in the first chapter is clearly the great-grandmother of a character I thought was unconnected. This character, introduced to amuse his maker—I am his maker—is full of meanness and tenderness, the key to the middle of the book. This dog knows the secrets of the family; this house has a hidden room; these characters were once married. The patterns don't feel like decisions: an intelligence greater than mine has put them in. Except I don't believe in an intelligence greater than mine, at least when it comes to my own fiction, and so I must accept that there's something working in parts of my brain that I don't have direct access to. My first job is to figure out the slantwise way I can get my subconscious to work. My second job is to, in revision, arrange the work so that the accidental patterns have the force of life.

As to the first: I picture my imagination as a dinghy attached to a dock. In order to write anything interesting, I have to unmoor it, let it drift, get swamped even, tilting closer to the depths at the center of the lake. Things that help me: those minutes in bed at night, after I have put my head down, when my thinking becomes biddable, just before I divine the surreal spinning blade of the dreamworld come to cut my thoughts to bits. Perhaps I'll write about the fashion shows my grandmother put on at her store, small-town Iowa outside, teenage girls in elegant taffeta inside, walking among the racks, here is a dress patterned with flowers, and top hats, and deviled eggs, and gallbladders—ah, a dream. Back it up, back it up.

In museums, I look at every canvas, read every caption, wander, thinking, *I wish I were a painter*, or *I want to watch a circus in Vienna in the late 1920s* or *I want to write something that's the equivalent of red flecked with green to make up a whole audience*, until my brain converts the longing into thoughts about fiction.

I love new independent bookstores, but as one who toils in the mines of bookage, they also make me anxious. Am I on a table? Am I face out? Am I there at all? All bookstores are beautiful; no bookstore is truly beautiful that doesn't stock my books. A good used bookstore, though, takes me out of the equation. They are monuments to persistence. They make me want to write.

Live music. Recorded music as I do something else with my body. Poetry readings; reading poetry. Long drives. Long swims and walks. Anything that calms the front of my brain and engages the back might open the aperture.

It's changed over my life. It will change for you, too.

118 | WE ARE LUCKY: THE WRITTEN WORD IS THE MOST durable of all art. Weather can't touch it. It needs no maintenance. It holds up even to reproduction: ten thousand copies, and it's still itself.

119 | UNDERSTANDING MY CHARACTERS IS A COMBINATION of improvisation and apprehension. By *improvisation*, I mean a lot of knowledge and no concrete thought: I follow the line of my sentences and find my characters that way. I don't think, *This is just a first draft; it can be awful.* I think, *Listen to that: it sounds right.* I want it to be beautiful; I am paying attention to logic that rises up from the writing itself.

By *apprehension*, I mean all three definitions of the word: *understanding*, *uncertainty*, *arrest*. I want to perceive the character the way I might an interesting real-life person, through a process that surprises me and deepens. I don't want to be fooled; or, I only want to be fooled at the start, as I fall in love. But are the characters really who they seem to be? Eventually I say, *Halt. Hold still. Look me in the eye, if only for a moment. Sit with me, though I understand you don't want to, I understand you want to move through this world without interference. I am your creator, and my job is to interfere.*

120 | IN EARLY DRAFTS, A CHARACTER'S BAD HABITS can become the short story's bad habits: a tendency to prevaricate, protect, digress, avoid the one thing they should think about. Characters need to have bad habits to be hu-

man; later drafts make sure that those bad habits don't drive the story.

121 THERE ARE ALL SORTS OF PLEASURABLE, SNEAKY ways to develop characters that have nothing to do with biographical detail or physical description. Describing delusions or obsessions as they happen is one. Knowing what clothing they wear—knowing their feelings about clothing altogether. Their relationship to driving: Do they like it? Are they reckless, inattentive? Think of the things you know about yourself that feel essential but never make it into conversation: the width of your feet; under what circumstances you will wear a hat; your interest in amusement parks; what sort of room you feel most physically comfortable in; your taste in music, especially the awful songs of adolescence that move you to tears.

122 I HAVE NO STRONG FEELINGS ABOUT WHETHER writers should describe their characters physically. This is a basic aesthetic choice. Some writers want readers to know what color their characters' eyes are. Some absolutely do not. Your characters may appear to you as a gesture, an unusual way of holding themselves that makes you wonder, *Who are you?* You might be a writer who sees their characters cinematically, every expression and gesture, or you might never see more than the back of a head.

123 | I DON'T KNOW WHAT MY OWN CHARACTERS look like, really, apart from their dimensions, which I know to the inch and the ounce. If I try I can see more, a faded snapshot in which the bill of a baseball cap or a quirk of orange light obscures faces. I know the quality of their hair, the color of their eyes, gestures, particular facial expressions—again, glimpsed as though in a photo album, familiar people you can't believe were ever that young. (It might be worth mentioning that, while I'm not entirely faceblind, my powers of recognition are comically bad. Midsemester, I once accused a stranger of taking a chair in a class I was teaching, then realized he was a student I knew well who had gotten a not-particularly-drastic haircut. This is one story out of thousands.)

What I know about my characters—what I feel in my own limbs and torso—is proximity. I know how tall and broad they are in relation to one another and how that makes them feel. Who is standing, who is sitting, how close. The heat coming off them. How that changes things.

124 | IN GRADUATE SCHOOL WE WERE TAUGHT THAT short stories were apprentice work for novels. This is like saying that tap dance is apprentice work for the tango. I'm ashamed at how entirely I believed this, despite knowing that some brilliant novelists never write a single short story, stories being a much more recent invention; plenty of geniuses of the story form never write a novel.

There is no life drawing in fiction, no practicing of scales: there's only writing bad work until you write something good. No platonic ideal of a short story, though it will seem to you as though there is: a story comes to you. In your head it's the best story you've ever written, perhaps the best story of all time. (You haven't started writing it yet.) You begin to convert it into sentences. Soon you have a sinking feeling. This isn't the story in your head. It can't be: that story was made of pixie dust and the souls of the dead and maybe one really fine opening line, which you realize now has nothing to do with the story itself. If you're lucky, you'll realize your conundrum a third of the way through the first draft, though for some of us the awful realization kicks in a third of a page down. The best thing to do is get to the end, and to reckon with your disappointments and possibilities in revision.

125 THE GREATEST DIFFERENCE BETWEEN NOVELS and short stories is in character. We spend so much more time with novel characters and they are—should be—larger and deeper in every way. This is the reason a writer should ignore the inevitable readerly reaction to an excellent story that has a lot of characters and takes place over a number of years: *This should be a novel!* No, it shouldn't. The characters won't make it. It's like organ transplantation. A small heart is a good heart, but you cannot put it in a large body and expect it to do the job. Many bad novels have been written out of terrific stories. Conversely, a failed short story can turn into a great novel.

Even vivid short story characters possess a mere thimbleful of the animating spirit of an actual human. Novel characters: a cup and a half. The dullest actual human being is more complicated than the most complex fictional character, fuller of contradiction, fuller of love and hate and every intermediary emotion between.

126 ONCE I WROTE A NOVEL MERELY BECAUSE I HAD time on my hands and some momentum: I was on sabbatical and I'd finished a collection of short stories. As I recall, this novel featured pleasant descriptions of furniture and clothing, as well as a museum guard who stole from his museum—one of those things I've always meant to write about—but the major characters were the size of short story characters. I hadn't sat with them: they just showed up, and I didn't have enough time to be puzzled by them. A child prodigy, of course. Children's television. An extremely tall woman. Hats. But the novel's lungs were too small to breathe on their own. This is the fourth of my unpublished novels. My first unpublished novel was similarly conceived out of spare time and not enough thought. I had five weeks and wrote a book just to see if I could, and I remember nothing about it other than a character wore a mouse-brown hat with a mouse-gray band (a detail I've put elsewhere in fiction). I don't think the five-week book

exists in any form anywhere on this earth; only one person read it, and her reaction was so lukewarm it still hurts. Lukewarm was a kindness.

127 IN FIRST DRAFTS, WE WRITE AS LOVING PARENTS to our characters. We want them to make their own interesting mistakes, to be able to function in the world, but also we instinctively protect them from the worst of the world. We indulge them and let them develop. We want what's good for them.

In later drafts, we should be unforgiving gods, to do not what's good for the single character but for the world itself, which is often at direct odds with what's good for the character. The character will be fine—memorable and believable, despite being hurt or killed—because of earlier care.

Being an unforgiving god allows you to revise with pleasure. You can ruin people's lives, for the sake of the story.

Characters, like writers, must fail. It's difficult, when you love them. You want to protect them, and if they have the stuff of life, *they* don't want to fail or be hurt or humiliated. You will find yourself writing scenes in which something serious is about to go down, and the character leaves. Just walks out of the room to look out a window and *think*. Avoids the conversation or the argument, as human beings are wont to do. (Fictional characters are often looking out windows. I don't know why; I suppose it seems contemplative.)

128 | BABY BOOKS, THE SOCIAL SECURITY NAME DAtabase, the names of authors on your bookshelf, thin air, childhood classmates, old phone books, graveyards: plenty of ways to come up with character names. Some writers like some flash and oddity and some absolute plainness. What is statistically unusual is not unrealistic—that's true about anything in fiction, not just names—but that won't convince some blockheads. Some blockheads believe that *realistic fiction* is that which is demographically most usual—or, worse, that which is demographically most usual *in fiction itself*. Realism in fiction, like most things, is a spectrum, and there's no need for a reader to instantly know where on the spectrum a story is, as long as it's obeying, as always, its own rules. All fiction is a construct: real life, *fiction vérité*, would be intolerable. (There's a lot of fiction that's pretty close; I find it intolerable.)

Naming a child or naming a character can come with the same anxieties and pleasure, the worry about suitability and the pleasure of finding something both euphonious and evocative. With characters, unlike children, you can change a name without permission when they're quite grown-up. For one of my novels, I took names from a family genealogy, and there was one character I was calling Jack who just wouldn't come clear. Then I looked back at the genealogy and saw that the actual person's first name was Joe, and I made it right, and that worked. I knew him. This is as close to mysticism as I get: he was never meant to be Jack. He was always Joe deep down.

129 IF YOUR CHARACTERS ALL LOOK ONE WAY, AND you insert a character who looks another way—race, weight, disability, age—who is only referred to by a salient visual quality: don't. That's the first step in writing about difference: don't use somebody else's difference to turn them into an object in your story, mere decoration. You don't need to write long pages on the souls of every person walking down your fictional streets, but it's useful to perceive any character as somebody with a soul and not just an exterior, even if your main characters can't. Indeed, if you write about somebody demographically different than you, you should be able to write that character from the inside out, not rain down character attributes that cling to the exterior. If you are not inside a character, understanding what choices they're making and why, the character will not be able to make their own decisions. You will not know what they think, you will only guess, guess again, keep guessing.

130 WHETHER OR NOT TO WRITE ABOUT AND FROM THE point of view of people who are demographically different from you is one of those complicated questions that people want to answer definitively. To vote on, nearly. Yes, you should do it, because nothing human is alien, and trying to decide what makes a person too different, too other from you—age? Race? Gender?—is an ugly process. No, you shouldn't, because the stories of marginalized people have been stolen by people in power for as long as stories have been written down, stolen for profit and propaganda, twisted to justify oppression. Yes, you can, but you should ask somebody from the community you're writing about to vet your work, see if you've got it right. No, it's colonial work, insidious and interior. Yes, you can, as long as you do it well and are open to criticism. No, there are some experiences that a fiction writer can neither know nor make up, and to try to do so will trivialize the entire existence of actual, living, harmed people. Yes, because a novel populated by only one sort of person out of caution alone has nothing to say about the complexities of being alive and ends up being a form of accidental science fiction no matter what the aimed-for genre.

It's such a complex question that it feels like guidance and expertise could help. There are excellent essays on this subject, and if it's a question you're interested in, you should read them all, and then work up your own philosophy, and write your work, or don't. It's important to know that you might do it badly.

You might do it badly. This is something I say to students, when they ask me unanswerable questions. Then, *There's only one way to find out.*

If they have a stomach for failing, they try. Sometimes they fail.

131 | MY SECOND NOVEL WAS IN THE VOICE OF A MAN, a character based on a relative I'd never met whose photographs intrigued me. He was the right person to tell the story. I didn't even think about it. At a reading, somebody

said to me that she thought it was brave of me to write from the point of view of a man. I laughed and said that if I'd thought of it as brave, I wouldn't have started.

"I couldn't do it," she said. "I don't understand men."

I don't understand men, either, or human beings of any gender, or any category. The one man, this single human—the fictional fellow I made up by examining photographs of my great-great-uncle Mose as a young man—him I understood, *because* I made him up. Even now I understand him better than I understand myself. (I don't particularly understand myself.) Probably I became a writer to fathom other people, fathom in the sense of dropping a weight inside to see how deep they go.

This really *is* a moment when I'm talking to myself: I only write about people unlike me when, after a mixture of research and thought, I feel as though I understand the character. Not their entire demographic; not every single person of their circumstances, age, gender, race, religion, economic situation, time, place. Just this one person, plus a relative or two, a friend. My *feeling* might be based on ignorance, a genuine inability to take everything into account. A reader who more closely resembles the character might decide I've got it entirely wrong. That's the bargain I make when I write: I have total control (even if it doesn't feel like control) only in composition.

132 | RESEARCH SUGGESTS THAT COMPASSION AND empathy use different parts of the brain, and that com-

passion is more useful. People who are empathetic to the suffering of others can feel paralyzed by that suffering, whereas if they feel compassion—if they can recognize suffering without taking on the pain of it—they're capable of helping.

Kindness is an overrated quality in a fiction writer. So is ruthlessness. An interest in all of humanity is useful.

133 | MY STUDENTS JOKE ABOUT HOW OFTEN I TALK about physicality. I'm tiresome on the subject. Writers can become so compelled by the inner lives of their characters that they, the characters, become like fireflies trapped in jars. By *fireflies*, I mean *souls*, though I am not religious. By *jars*, I mean heads.

Attention is given from the neck up. We see the world only when a character looks at it. We may even be aware of the point-of-view character turning their head to look around. If another character comes into the room, and the character isn't looking in their direction, we hear a disembodied voice.

(By the way: nobody has ever heard a voice say something and turned to see that it is somebody they are well acquainted with, e.g.:

> "I think that dog is dead," a voice behind me said. I turned my head. It was my mother.

That isn't how voices or mothers work.)

Nor do you need to write about The Body, what it means to own one, especially an unruly body. That might be your topic—it's one of mine—but it's not essential.

134 WHEN YOUR POINT-OF-VIEW CHARACTER IS stuck in their head, they may only be able to see other characters from the neck up, resulting in a lot of eye work—brows raised, one eyebrow raised, brows furrowed; squinting, winking, blinking to convey emotion, slowly, rapidly, twice, once. Characters roll their eyes, especially while talking. Eye contact becomes momentous: making it, avoiding it, breaking it. Characters gaze, spot, spy, look, peer, gawp.

Sometimes the mouth gets involved—smiling, grinning, frowning (and here I bring possibly startling news: in the US frowning is something you do with your mouth, and in the UK something you do with your eyebrows). A character might bite a lip, or purse both lips. Sometimes it's humor-related: chuckling, chortling, sniggering, smirking, giggling, laughing. The story seems to occur in a nitrous oxide leak.

135 WHEN YOUR CHARACTERS LOOK AT SOMETHING, including one another, consider describing what they see instead.

He looked discombobulated. *His goatee was in disarray.* I looked at my mother. *My mother felt her jaw tentatively, as though it belonged to someone else.* She looked out the window. *Across the street, the neighbor children were burying what looked like a tattered pot roast.*

When it becomes impossible to get a character to cross a room—a common affliction in fiction—it's because the character hasn't had a body all story, they've just been thinking big thoughts and running their mouth, and now they have to move, only to find their entire carcass has fallen asleep. They wonder—you wonder—how it's done, relocating this awkward human mechanism. They look down. Their whole body has pins and needles. Their hands move like a marionette's.

136 | IF YOU'RE TOO INSIDE A CHARACTER'S HEAD and not body, then character and not place becomes the sole setting for the work. (Your character's head *is* a setting; so is your character's body.) No matter the amusement parks or palaces the character walks through, they cannot get out of themselves. You have to do that through physicality.

The only way out of the head is through the body. All the way through.

137 | WHEN I SPEAK OF PHYSICALITY, I MEAN AN INtermittent acknowledgment of gravity and the factual world around the characters. Practice periodic visualization. Stop and see. Note whether anything surprises you.

Pull yourself into your characters' bodies, I tell my students, not so that they become more conscious of the physical, but less, so that characters are integrated people, and not highly evolved worms piloting complicated blood-and-bone robots. Your main character is a human being—

(that is, if your main character *is* a human being; you may want to write about science-fiction worms piloting complicated robots, in which case you will probably find this writing manual useless)

—your main character is a human being on the same planet as other human beings, connected by the curve of that planet. If you don't know what a character should do, put yourself in the character's body. Often that alone will tell you. We may think that emotion comes out of our heads or torsos, and if we consult those spaces we will understand *what next*. But as often our characters' humanity exists in their hips and elbows. The backs of their knees; the small of their backs.

Thinking of a character's physicality is just another way to see. In an odd way, it can make a character's body disappear, or a character's estrangement from and therefore awareness of their body disappear. (Estrangement and awareness aren't opposites. They're close to synonyms.)

In real life, too. Some days, I don't know what I think or feel, and then I realize that my self, or sense of self, or consciousness, has come unfixed from my body, is floating inches away, untended. I pull it back in; then I can think more clearly.

138 | GESTURE IS EVIDENCE THAT YOUR CHARACTERS exist: readers see and believe in them. A gesture that's unusual can even make a reader physically mimic it, book in lap. Gestures are communication from one character to another, if they're having trouble talking. Give your characters something do, and the charge between them will change. Pruning roses, burying a body, cooking a meal, sex, seeing a play, performing a play, seated next to each other at a dinner party, sitting across from each other at same.

139 | HUMAN BODIES ARE VARIOUS. YOUR OWN HUMAN body simultaneously has nothing to do with who you are—we are not defined by who we are physically—and everything to do with who you are—what we find difficult or easy to do shapes us; so does how other people see, judge, assume. It's easy to default in fiction to the physically average, or, worse, the particularly good-looking (fictional mothers are always suspiciously beautiful). On the human plane, each body has its own shape; there's no such thing as a "shapely" body in the same way there is no such thing (no matter what anyone says) as a "shapely" short story. The world is more interesting when a variety of human and fictional forms are acknowledged.

140 | DON'T DEFAULT TO THE ORDINARY OR AVERAGE in fiction altogether. If either is your subject, yes: you'll

find meaning in the ordinary and average, and strangeness there, too, because even the seemingly ordinary are very strange indeed, and no human being is ever truly average, *average* being a mathematical term, not a human one. No default average plot is interesting, no average language (which can too easily mean clichés that you don't notice are clichés, like *blood-curdling*). If you're tempted to think of yourself as ordinary—think of the things you'd be horrified for other people to know about you, your genuine hidden freakishness, the most inexplicable thing you did as a teenager. Something you've never told anyone, or nearly nobody. Then give that kink or shameful secret to a character. Who'll know? Only you. That's what fiction is for.

141 | THE BODY IS A FACT: LET CHARACTERS REACT TO facts. Fiction could do with a little more farting: every fart is a surprise, a failure, a joke, an event. I say that knowing that there are readers and writers who can't abide what they might call bathroom humor. I once received a rejection note from *The Paris Review* that described my "scatology" as "uninteresting." Not all of my advice is helpful.

142 | PERHAPS YOU HAVE THE OPPOSITE PROBLEM. You're not interested in, as it is sometimes called, *interiority*—that is, the internal world of your characters. (I don't know what most things are called in fiction, being a writer and not a scholar; I am, as a colleague once suggested of creative writers in a literature department, an amoeba teaching in a biology lab.) Not the soul for me, you might insist: I want to write about the intersection of my characters and the world; I want to reveal my characters through dialogue and action. Fair enough. It's even more important to know your characters from the inside, not necessarily thoughts, emotions, daydreams, but the part of their humanity that steers their bodies no matter how that body moves through space. You don't need to write about it. You just need to know it.

143 IN WORK UNCONCERNED WITH INTERIORITY, hearts rise in throats, jump, drop to stomachs, speed up, slow down, beat, beat, beat. Scalps crawl. Autonomic bodily reactions, visible only on the surface of the skin: flushing, blushing, gooseflesh, hair prickling on the backs of necks. Blood runs cold or slow. A great attention is paid to breath: characters breathe slowly or deeply or shallowly, or become aware of their breathing. Stomachs jump or roil or make characters sick, nauseated. None of these are real actions. They fail to describe. They change nothing and show nothing.

How does this manifest? I write in the margins of student work. *Let us see.*

Or hear or smell. Or taste! Nothing yanks a character into their physical self like a taste of soup, delicious or acrid, room temperature or scalding hot.

144 SETTING IS A KIND OF CONTOUR MAP, WITH THE central, highest point the soul:

Soul, anatomy, body, clothing, furniture, room, building, street, neighborhood, municipality, state, country, continent, hemisphere, planet, galaxy. (All of this tailored to your actual setting.) Geography, weather. Time deserves to be in there, a concentric set of steps: moment, hour, time of day, day of the week, time of month, month, season, year, decade, century, epoch. You needn't keep in mind of all these circles of time and space, but they surely exist in rings around your characters. Knowing that helps me, especially if I get stuck.

Clothing is setting, extremely local. Every day we make sartorial decisions that reveal who we are. Every day, we extract information about strangers from their clothes. The slovenly, the dapper, the eccentric, the conformist, the athletic, the sedentary, the ambitious. A well-dressed character is a jolt of pleasure for readers, just as well-described food is.

145 I WAS ABOUT TO SAY THAT IN MY EXPERIENCE, people don't talk enough about setting, but my experience is extremely limited. I last took a fiction writing class in the spring of 1990, before the turn of the century. Otherwise, I only know the classes I teach, plus some rumors about my colleagues. It irritates me when I hear people complaining about how writing workshops work, or how writing is taught, when mostly what they know about it is their own experience, good or bad, as a student. When I began to teach, I took some things from my important teachers, dropped other things. Then I kept changing my tactics: what was important to me shifted, and what was important to the students themselves. Young people are different today than they were thirty years ago, when I was a grad student; and we were different from young people thirty years before that. Young people are part of society, which is always changing. Teaching graduate students and undergraduates allows me to swim in those changes, to encounter them early, an enormous influence on my own writing and my humanity.

Can you imagine sitting down in your college classes, only to meet somebody who comported themselves like a frosh from your parents' time? True enough, it's a flaw and superpower of youth to believe that their standards—their beliefs and morals and ways of thinking about themselves in relation to one another—are advanced just because they are recent. It's a flaw of the middle-aged to believe that their beliefs and morals are correct because they've been tested by time. Whatever age you are, you find reasons to conclude that your own beliefs are true. That's the human condition, too.

146 | THINK OF SETTING AS CONTEXT. IT SHOULDN'T be happenstance. If you're not interested in the interiors of houses, pick a floor plan of a place you know well. Like the characters' bodies, you don't need to describe it, but if

you can picture them they will be able to use their bodies to walk around. They won't float down hallways like cosmonauts; you won't have to come up with a sofa only when they need to sit down, an end table so they have somewhere to put down a drink. When they go outside, it's good to know what they will encounter, trees or asphalt, strangers or horses. None of this needs to be specified. If you have a sense of what space a character is moving through, your readers will, too, even if you do not mention so much as a mantelpiece or a creek.

147 | I WOULD LIKE TO OFFER YOU A MINDFULNESS exercise, but I know nothing about mindfulness. I can offer only an awkwardness exercise, a self-consciousness exercise.

For each step, as much as possible, don't think of words, but sensations. Close your eyes, at least metaphorically or from time to time.

Imagine somebody, a stranger, walking into the room. Concentrate your attention in the top of your head.

Remember a headache you've had, or an earache. Think about at what angle you held your head to accommodate that pain. Move your attention to your face. Think about the last time somebody told you something you didn't want to hear. Take on that expression. Try to feel it from the inside.

Down into your neck, your shoulders. Think of a physical activity that uses your shoulders, your arms: sport, chore, manual work, acts of sex or love. Bowling or cello playing or washing the dishes or carrying a child or changing the oil in your car. How does that feel? See how your arms are held. Does the activity use one arm more than the other? Is it painful, pleasurable, both? Feel it down to your elbows, your forearms, your wrists. In your head, stop the activity. Hold still. Put your attention in your hands. How do they feel? What might you do to change the way they feel?

Come back to your torso, down to your waist. Remember an article of clothing, now lost, that was meaningful to you. It could be an unlikely jacket that made you feel wonderful, or a uniform, or a dress you wore on a day that changed your life. Remember details: a wide collar, a zipper with a cold brass pull. In your mind put your hands in the pockets (deep? Shallow?) and let your posture shift. Feel your elbows and wrists, the fabric against your knuckles.

Bring your attention further down. Sit, if you're not already. Move your attention to your thighs, your knees. Think about the force of gravity even at your stillest moments. How does it feel to have to obey?

Think about the other people around you, wherever you are, in the room or in the building, or on the street walking on the sidewalk, in the next-door bungalow or six floors above you, in airplanes flying overhead. There is always somebody else present eventually.

Animals, too, inside or out, the squirrels and jays, the dogs being walked in the heat or chill or rain.

Down to your ankles, your feet, your toes. Think about the shoes all around your feet, the soles of your shoes on the floor. Let your attention flow through your feet to the ground. Bring yourself back to your whole body. You are in your clothing, in your chair. Feel the room around you. Now the building. Now the street, the neighborhood, the town, every pertinent geographic concentric shape, state or county or township, country, continent. You are an envelope addressed by a precocious child to your exact location. Think of a place that is not where you are but is important to you—think of its physical distance, and its physical connection to where you are now.

Back to your own body. A stranger walks into the room. What next?

148 NO, IT'S IMPOSSIBLE TO SEPARATE CHARACTER from plot from setting.

The body is the apparatus of plot. The body is what characters use to do things.

VII

149 LONG AGO I DECIDED THAT WRITERS WRITE FICtion very much the way they process the information of life itself, which in turn comes from childhood. If you had a childhood that was full of event, you were concerned with plot, because you learned at an early age that life was event. A childhood full of interesting people: character. A childhood full of arguments would show up in your work as surely as a childhood full of natural beauty.

It's an extraordinarily self-serving theory. I still believe in it.

150 ON THE FIRST DAY OF CLASS I SOMETIMES ASK students what they'd like to improve in their fiction. (It's always a good question; I just don't always remember to ask.) The most common answer is plot. *I'm no good at plot*, they say. *I'm not even sure I know what plot is.* I would have said this myself, once upon a time. Or, if I felt pretentious: *I'm not interested in plot.* I tried to hide my weaknesses with what I felt I was good at: description, character. My plots leaned on chronology. My characters mostly thought and

felt; they spent too much time indoors; they never said what was on their minds.

In those days I thought of plot as something like the music box mechanism inside a fancy stuffed animal, with a stiff boomerang key attached to a cylindrical fitting that went through the fur of the flank and into the gears. You'd wind it like a travel alarm clock. It didn't even animate the animal: it only played an ever-slower song. I was a snob about plot, as we are snobs about things that make us feel insecure.

151 THE THEORY THAT THERE ARE ONLY A HANDFUL of plots—a stranger comes to town, the hero goes on a quest, a fortune is made, overcoming a monster—doesn't help those of us confounded by plot, because these *aren't* plots: they're dull summaries of event. Event is what happens in a story, but plot is the electricity between events, how events lead one to the next, working the way through the characters. It's the difference between character and character development, between a line of dialogue and a conversation. Event is a particle of plot.

In any story—or novel, but it's clearer in a short story—there is an active plot, and an emotional plot. The active plot is made up of the events of the story, in the order they occur in the story. The emotional plot is made up of what the characters feel, in the order they feel them in the story.

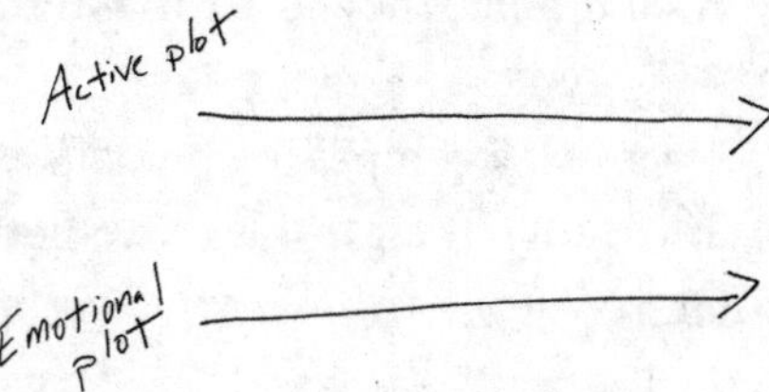

Where real, true plot occurs is where the active and the emotional interact, when event affects what characters feel, and what they feel affects what they do. It's not a one-to-one correspondence, *feel/act/feel/act*. But there's a charge between the two plots. This isn't science. It isn't even art. It's how I think of plot when I teach but not when I write.

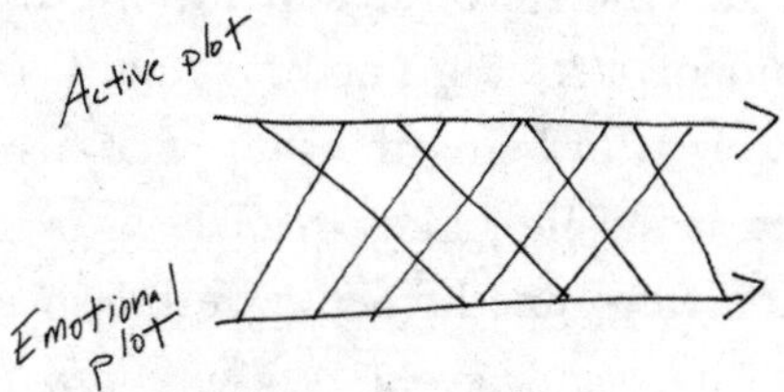

I draw the above chart when I've read something where there's some disconnect, when events don't seem to be happening to the characters, or when the characters don't enact the plot but merely endure it. If you have ever read a story that seems beautiful and is full of both emotion and event but feels fundamentally dead at its heart, it's because it has an emotional plot and an active plot that have nothing in common. They just run parallel to each other.

If you have ever met a compelling human being who is unknowable: same thing. Their insides have nothing to do with their outsides.

152 WHAT HAPPENS WHEN INNER LIFE MEETS OUTER life? That's the most interesting question in fiction. It's also the most important of human existence.

153 YOU HAVE A CHARACTER; THE CHARACTER HAS A secret; toward the end of the story the secret is revealed; the character, and therefore the story, is "solved." Childhood abandonment, a stillborn baby, regular beatings by a beloved—all worthy of being the subject of fiction rather than a trapdoor at the end, a key in a lock. My Lord, such plots bore me. Only superheroes have origin stories, in which a single cataclysmic event—rocketing to earth, witnessing the murder of your parents—explains every single thing that follows, and somehow necessitates great secrecy. If such a thing happens to an actual human, it's rare, and it isn't the *keeping* of the secret that forms somebody's whole subsequent personality.

In fiction, secrets are most compelling when a reader is in on them but the characters aren't. We know who Clark Kent is; that's the pleasure of it. It's only those dumb mortals on the page who are in the dark.

154 ONE OF THE REASONS THE WALKING-THROUGH-a-city-thinking-things plot is compelling if not timeworn is because the main character, taken out of context, is forced to have more interesting thoughts, just as an actual human is. If you construct a plot around travel—a transcontinental train ride, a one-day ramble—make sure that the two halves of the plot are interacting.

If plot eludes you, it can be useful to introduce events and locations and other characters that run counter to who the character is. Getting your character out of the house and into the world makes that easier.

155 WRITERS—EVERYONE, REALLY—SHOULD TRAVEL when they're young. In your twenties you can ride across the country on a train, sitting up all the way. You can drive for twelve hours straight. You have the time, anatomy, and willingness to fly to Iceland on four different flights with an eight-hour layover in Pittsburgh, all so you can travel on the cheap. And it's not that you tolerate the complications, you like them. When you turn thirty-five, something sad happens: you become delicate about travel. You are no longer delighted by the fleabag; you develop a preference for the most direct flight possible; on a long train ride you might pay extra for a better seat, or even spring for a little room with a fold-down bed. Apart from reading, there is no better training for being a writer than travel. I suppose it does broaden the mind—you learn about other cultures, your powers of empathy deepen—but mostly it takes you

out of your own context. Dislocation is helpful to a fiction-writing brain.

156 | I USED TO WRITE SHORT STORIES WITH NO IDEA of either plot or event, just what I wanted the characters to feel. These days I begin with event and setting; character comes afterward. For me, event is simultaneously primary and not all that important. Back when I confused plot and event, I thought that things that happened to the characters had to be of such significance that I struggled to think of anything good enough. Now I think, as long as *something* happens, that's all that matters.

What's important is the *effect* of the event, not the event itself: the light that is given off, not the light bulb. Plot is about consequence, even though human beings, as a species, are notoriously incredulous about cause and effect.

These days I know most corners of a short story before I start, except what the characters feel, which comes as a surprise.

157 | FOR SHORT STORIES, NEARLY EVERYTHING; FOR novels, astonishing ignorance. I step onto a road in the dark; I cannot see the road except by my flashlight, which is composed of sentences. The route is already there; the sentences reveal it. When I stall it's because I'm at a fork in that road. Which way? It doesn't matter, if I pay attention to my character.

158 | A SHORT STORY IS LIKE ONE OF THOSE LOST FAMily photographs you sometimes find in antique stores, people separated from their biographies, melancholy but compelling: Are those two people related, despite looking nothing alike? Why is she smiling? Why is he holding his ear? What's that weird building they're standing in front of? Is the hammered light because of a nearby body of water, or a flaw in the processing? To write a story, I need to paint my own version of the photograph, one that explicates some mysteries and leaves others intact.

A novel is like finding an enormous filthy canvas in an antique store. I know its dimensions. I can see a vague shape in the center. Writing the novel is cleaning the canvas. Everything is already there, though I can't see it. As I clean I see more. That figure in the front is a woman, not a man; there's a child standing next to her; but there are figures in the background, dozens, and they interest me, there's something off about them. *Tell me more*, I tell myself.

159 | HERE'S HOW I LEARNED TO WRITE FICTION. IN college I submitted a very terrible story to the literary magazine. One of the editors suggested I might join the Boston University Literary Guild (pronounced *bulge*), which was run by glamorous, smoking, swearing upperclassmen who made erudite dirty jokes. In high school, I had wanted to be the best writer by vanquishing everyone else, or by not trying at all and assigning myself the title of *best* in my heart. I could not vanquish the writers of Bulge, so instead

I worshipped them. They were mostly poets; I tried to be a poet. I took poetry classes. When an older student told me he was taking the graduate playwriting course and suggested that I submit for the next semester, I wrote a play and, much to my shock, got in.

Before playwriting, I'd never thought about the practical side of a piece of writing. I would have claimed I liked writing *because* there were no practical aspects. In playwriting class, we went over and over the work out loud, reading each other's plays. Occasionally professional actors came in. The actors and my professor and my classmates didn't critique: they asked reasonable questions. *Didn't this guy order pancakes fifteen minutes ago? Where are they? Why are there fifteen people in this one-act play? Could it be staged with five more meaningfully? Why is nobody interrupting this jerk? Why isn't anybody reacting to what that lady just said? This character I'm playing, tell me: He the sort of guy who cheats on his wife?*

Playwriting class took the work out of my body, so I could see it. See that it was capable of standing away from me; see what its actual deficiencies were, visible at the uncanny literal distance. Then I could try to fix them for the next read-through.

Good writing comes from inside you, is organ-like in its way, necessary, vital. Then you have to look at it in the light of day.

Because I was new to playwriting and poetry, I never felt dumb. Even now it feels vain to say that I was surprisingly good for a teenaged amateur, which is not to say good. In poetry I experimented; in playwriting I paid attention to structure, architecture, tension.

Playwriting didn't come naturally to me, ambivalent about collaboration as I was and remain. When I heard people speak lines I had written, I believed they were stressing the wrong syllables.

I loved poetry. Mostly I wrote persona poems about two of my obsessions, Catholic saints and twentieth-century American mobsters. Poetry taught me about compression, elision, how to contract and expand in a small space. I understood structure in a new way, being able to look at it from above. Poems are multidirectional; I hoped fiction could be, too.

160 AS I WROTE POETRY AND PLAYS, I WROTE A LOT of terrible stories. This isn't modesty. My technically realist stories had no interest in real life; my characters were all voice and no body. When I wrote fiction, I still cared too much what people thought, and I believed I knew what I was doing, and I did it with a lot of force. My sentences were the equivalent of the baby sweater I would later knit in a frenzy: I was so intent on making a thing I left no air, no space for interpretation. I wrote sentences meant to thwart or confuse or placate the imaginary reader over my shoulder.

I don't think it's a coincidence that I've given up poetry, playwriting, everything, for fiction.

Maybe it wasn't writing the actual poetry that helped my fiction. Maybe it was reading about saints and gangsters. If you come to fiction because of an innate interest in human character, you might write fiction that answers the question, *How did this character get this way?* That was the plot of all my early stories.

Much better to ask: *Given that a character is this way, what do they do?*

They endure arrows for the sake of their faith. They put on hair shirts or ascend to the rafters of a church to escape the smell of sinful human bodies. They kill a guy and tie his corpse to a pinball machine but forget to perforate the stomach, filled with the buoyant gases of human existence, so the corpse comes floating up to the surface of the river.

VIII

161 | I LIED WHEN I SAID I KNOW NOTHING BEFORE I start writing a novel. Before the first sentence, I've decided on a structure, a general shape, and some architectural elements to hold it up: the size of the book and its constituent parts (chapters, sections, how many of both); the stretch of time the book will cover; how many points of view; any other narrative tricks.

It's helpful to know these things ahead of time. The writing itself is cake batter—you can adjust and add, but you need to know whether you're making a sheet cake or cupcakes, a layer of cake of equal or graduated layers. Good to get your pans out and ready, move the racks in the oven, so you can think a little about the final object.

I lied because I'm always certain about my structural decisions, and always wrong. The work I think is going to be entirely chronological and contemporary turns out to be historical with a contemporary frame; the little novel four hundred pages long; the experimental novel, not at all. You would think I'd learn a lesson, but when it comes to my own fiction I'm ineducable (probably why I like teaching; everyone's not like me), and believe with all my heart that this time I have it figured out. No parts to *this* novel. Twenty chapters, each ten pages long. Ten chapters, each twenty pages long. A novel that takes place in a single day, each chapter a block of time. A novel that takes place over exactly a century, twenty pages a decade. I'm always wrong.

162 FOR INSTANCE, UNTIL THE FINAL DRAFT, MY last novel had an auxiliary narrative in the form of a writing manual, a running commentary on the novel proper. I kept tinkering with placement, footnotes or endnotes or marginalia. (Such notes are a structure; they change the shape of narrative.) The book was by far the most autobiographical fiction I'd ever written; I had to fool myself into doing it. In the ersatz manual, I critiqued and disparaged and undermined my fiction. Oh, I was clever, I thought, sincere in my soul (the narrative) and snarky in my exoskeleton (the notes).

In the end, it didn't work. The snarkiness of the voice was abrasive and had no through line. About 10 percent of the notes—maybe—I folded into the novel. I retained a single footnote and realized it was the reason I had wanted footnotes at all. *Can a book have a single footnote?* you might wonder, and my answer is, *This book has a single footnote.* (That's my answer to nearly any question about fiction that starts *Can a book . . . ?*: This one does. Similarly in fiction classes I'm baffled when somebody says, "I don't believe this character would do this." It betrays a curious lack of imagination in a writer. What do you mean you don't believe the character would do such a thing? The character just did.)

Some structures turn out to be scaffolding, indispensable in construction, extraneous at the end. You take it away to find a complete edifice with an internal structure—loadbearing walls, vaulted ceilings—that allows the novel or story to stand alone. Sometimes structure is a trellis upon which you have trained roses, and cannot be removed without collapse.

My footnotes were scaffolding, or perhaps a series of jacks that held the earlier drafts up. There is no way I could have written the book without them. With them in place, I fooled myself into writing an autobiographical novel, and, simultaneously or consecutively, the craft book you have before you.

163 | A FOOL'S GAME TO TRY TO SEPARATE THE ELEMENTS of fiction. Anything that repeats in your work is structure: an image, a chapter size, sentence length, paragraphing, punctuation. A running joke. A first-person narrator running through an entire book is a structure; three different first-person narrators (whether they repeat or appear as solid blocks) is a different kind. A changing point of view and how it moves and shapes the book is structural.

Suspense is structural. It's even an architectural word. Like the cables of a suspension bridge, running from one side to the other: it holds a book up. The question is not why a gun on the mantelpiece at the start of Act One has to go off by the end of Act Three, but why it is on the mantelpiece in the first place: to threaten. That threat runs through the play. A banister, a ceiling beam.

164 I ONCE WROTE A NOVEL DRAFT WITH CHAPTERS of varying lengths, and when I outlined the book after having written the whole thing, as I am these days given to doing, I could see very clearly that in nearly every case I'd put the chapter break in the wrong place, and once I'd rechaptered the book the chapters were all about fifteen pages after all. Structure can be subconscious, too, turns out.

(My post-draft outlines are all narrative paragraphs about what happens in each chapter, a way to get another angle on the book. I still can't figure out the outline form.)

Another time I wrote a 450-page long novel without any chapter breaks at all, thinking I would put them in later, which turned out to be possible but unpleasant. Chapter breaks are a form of punctuation, and they shape your book the way other punctuation shapes your sentences. They are a way to put both structure and air into your work. Some writers are consistent in their chapter lengths and methods; some change book to book.

165 SOME PUBLISHED BOOKS SCARCELY HAVE PARAGRAPH breaks: this, like all punctuation, is a matter of style. A book with very few paragraphs or chapter breaks asks a

lot of its readers; you must reward them for that sort of sustained attention. A book in which most of the paragraphs are a sentence or two long can feel exhausting in a different way, as though the driver is continually tapping the brakes. Perhaps the opinion that most marks me as an old fogey is my disapproval of the newish popularity of what is either lyric essay or internet paragraphing, in which there is no indenting and a double space after every single paragraph. I hate profligate double spacing as much as other people hate immoderate exclamation points: when you use a piece of punctuation reflexively, it loses its particular power.

166 | PUNCTUATION, FROM WEAKEST TO STRONGEST: comma, colon, parenthesis, hyphen, en dash, em dash, semicolon, period, exclamation point, question mark, paragraph break, double space, double space with a typographical element, chapter break on the same page, chapter break on a different page, chapter break with a number, chapter break with a title, part break. Books written in series have meta punctuation. This isn't scientific. You may classify otherwise.

167 | I LOVE A SPACE BREAK, AS YOU CAN TELL, FOR ITS particular powers. Having a hard time moving a character through time and space? Hit return twice: begin in the new time and space on the other side. It's a thrill for readers to make that leap. There is *meaning* in the gap. Frag-

mentary books—this is one, sort of—allow for the same work in a reader. What does this fragment have to do with that fragment? When you put them side by side, a little space between them, the reader does the work. *This, therefore that.* The reader supplies the *therefore.* Double spacing can turn your text into blocks, the sort that built the pyramids, held together not by mortar or joinery or steel rods but by their own weight, and by the work, the effort, of the reader. It can be a solider structure than attaching things through explanation.

168 I OFTEN SUGGEST THAT WRITERS CUT EXPLANATORY conjunctions and adverbs in fiction: *but*, *because*, *therefore*, *since.* Such words point out meaning; losing them paradoxically imbues the language with meaning, because the reader supplies it.

> She didn't want to go because she had a headache.
>
> She didn't want to go. She had a headache.
>
> My son has been traveling the Baltic states for six months now without a phone call but I know he loves me very much.
>
> My son has been traveling the Baltic states for six months now without a phone call. I know he loves me very much.

When a reader gets to supply the connection between the two thoughts, there's a little jounce of pleasure. We feel closer to the character: we know something they don't.

169 | ANY BELOVED PUNCTUATION CAN BECOME A BAD habit, mannered, embarrassingly visible, but what delight there is in choosing what you love! Parentheses, em dashes, colons. Even comma splices, which every good copy editor will wish to cure you of. Punctuation is a way to get your reader to hear the music of your prose. Not every piece is written in the same key or with the same time signature.

170 | ANYTHING THAT IS VISUAL IN FICTION IS A structure. Poets are used to thinking about what their work looks like: negative space, line breaks, indentation, punctuation, italics, the visual being the first introduction to anything on a page in any genre. Fiction, too: density of paragraphing, inclusion or absence of certain punctuation (commas, quotation marks), long runs of dialogue (whether narrow down the page or a fat expansive monologue), a legion of first-person pronouns—*I*, *I*, *I*. A reader sees these things. Writing itself is synesthetic: writing sounds and appears and means, if finding meaning is a sense. I think it is.

171 | ITALICS ARE SEEN BEFORE THEY'RE FELT, FELT before they're heard, whether used for emphasis in dialogue

—I don't *like* it; *I* don't like it; I *don't* like it—or to indicate a certain dreaminess, or dialogue heard from another room. Don't overuse italics, I tell my students, running a line of my own italics over my upper lip. Italics are satin. They are a sensory pleasure. Also nonstick: beautiful as they are, eventually meaning slides from them.

Based on my own research, 73 percent of readers skip or skim anything longer than an italicized sentence. This figure, like all my statistics, is entirely made up. In long passages, italics are typographical Teflon; the eye won't stick to them, and the brain decides an italicized passage is optional. Prologues in italics are especially slick and skippable. (I don't mind front matter in novels. I dislike the word *prologue*, which feels like a tag on a mattress that says that it cannot be ripped off under penalty of law: *This is essential; you'll have to take my word for that.* Too often a prologue is a way to avoid starting a novel.)

172 | IF YOU LOVE ITALICS, DON'T FIGHT ME. EMBRACE them. Explain to yourself what they do in your work and you will earn them.

173 | IF YOU SUFFER FROM A BLOCK OF ANY KIND—IF, for instance, you can't even think of a title, never mind a good one, never mind the right one, it helps to generate as many as you can. Some will be laughable, and the laughable ones will lead to something interesting. Event can work this way, too: write at the top of a page, *What can happen next?* and then a list. Your first answers may involve extraterrestrials in a piece of fiction that previously has been entirely earthbound, but eventually you will write something plausible for the work, meaningful. I still do this; it works for me.

It's tempting to think you must come up with the right title or event or line of dialogue in one go. I blame computers. I love them, too, I compose most of my work on my laptop, and handwrite or use a typewriter only when stuck. I'm old enough—God, how tiresome, people who say, *I'm old enough* when they mean *I'm old*—to have lived through the advent of word processing. In high school I typed my work, or sometimes my mother did it for me, taking my handwritten drafts and touch-typing without looking at her hands, a skill I found as remarkable as spinning hay into gold. At some point I got a typewriter with a little screen: you typed a line, made sure it was without error, hit enter, and the daisy wheel, a spinning round element with type on its petals at the center of the machine, committed it to paper. The machine itself might have been called a word processor, for this was the 1980s, the age of food processors. Anything might be smoothed down for consumption by a spinning wheel.

Once personal computers came in, we writers thought the whole business was going to be easier. How changeable our work would be, how easy to edit! We wouldn't have to *literally* cut and *literally* paste; we could devote that time to art, fiddling and revising, moving enormous blocks of text, deleting and adding as we liked. Our alterations would never show. Our work would be seamless.

It didn't work that way.

One of my college professors, a typewriter man, said he felt sorry for us. "You guys type a line, and on the screen it already looks perfect, as though it can't be improved." I think of this all the time. (His typed letters of recommendation had margins so wide on all sides that they looked like postage stamps in the middle of the page, paltry and elegant.)

The problem is that it can feel, when you start what you think of as a first draft on a computer, as though you are also starting the final draft. The thing itself. A kind of stage fright occurs. It's not that you have to type the *next* sentence, but the *right* sentence. In this way everything can feel momentous, fingers over keyboard, no matter how many times you rename files and keep your old version on your computer. A writer has to fight against that seeming perfection, through handwritten drafts or reading work aloud or printing out and scrawling all over the page; or writing in a notes app, by its very nature temporary. You have to fool yourself.

174 | OF ALL THE "ELEMENTS" OF "FICTION," THE ONE that's trickiest to isolate is dialogue. Is dialogue character? Plot? Language? Structure?

All of these things.

175 IF YOU'RE WRITING DIALOGUE BETWEEN STRANGERS that's just zinging along it's possible they are only saying what you expect them to say. Don't let your dialogue become too generic in your wish to make it realistic; don't make it solely informational, characters talking for the sake of the plot. Actual people are always saying the strangest things. They wish to wound, persuade, shock, be heard, be understood. Talking is not an involuntary process.

Nor is it an enormous effort. If your characters can't bear to open their mouths, if they turn away from each other and bite their lips, thinking of what they might say but never do, they're more doll than human. Worse than that: they're boring.

Dialogue is the answer to any number of problems in fiction. A character you can't get close to? Let 'em talk. Dialogue characterizes, shows the odd way people put sentences together. A plot that's stalled? Dialogue is action; it's something characters do to each other.

176 IF YOU'RE STUCK IN YOUR CHARACTERS' HEADS, having them speak to each other can feel impossible. They don't want to say anything meaningful at all, or only things too aimed at Meaning. They feel disordered and socially anxious. What can they say that will be interesting enough, that will have the ring of truth without being expository? (*As you already know, Rupert . . .*)

How *do* people talk?

Maybe this is why a lot of fiction these days forgoes quotation marks. Quotation marks can feel like barbed-wire fences strung up high, which characters must climb over in order to speak. Some writers italicize all dialogue, a way to set it off while forgoing quotation marks. Some use dashes (as some Irish writers do, and as dialogue is punctuated in Spanish). Other writers swear off all demarcation around dialogue, typographical or punctuational, and must make clear by syntax what is dialogue and what narrative.

Dialogue without quotation marks can feel quite beautiful. Spring fed, flowing directly from character to character. It's how I compose all my dialogue, free of quotation marks, attribution, gesture. Not a name, not an adverb. Easier to get to the language centers of the characters that way. Let 'em talk. Usually I do this in a separate file: I want them to ramble, parry, listen, ignore, avoid, and buttonhole. I generate at least twice as much dialogue as I ever use.

Once I've composed the dialogue, I put the fences back up. Except now the quotation marks aren't fences. They're lenses: they pull into focus what my characters say, make the dialogue sharp. I add gesture and setting and physicality and verbs of attribution: *said*, *replied*, *asked*. For me this is what turns talk into dialogue. Quotation marks are awkward, as human beings are awkward, and they feel right for my characters.

177 THERE HAS BEEN A MOVEMENT IN GRADE schools—my undergraduates have suffered through it, my children, too—with the battle cry *Said is dead*, in which well-meaning, wrongheaded language arts teachers implore their students to use more descriptive language for attributing dialogue: bellowed, inquired, screamed, chortled, etc. I'm sympathetic—the descriptive power of verbs is easily overlooked—but this is perhaps the worst writing advice I know that is regularly offered. Ugly. Pointless. Readers don't perceive the attribution of dialogue as an action. They perceive it, and properly—again, dialogue is action; it's something characters do to each other—as punctuation. *He said, she said, they said, they asked.* The verbs are dull because they're not important.

Dialogue should to the best of its abilities describe itself; if you have to wait until the verb and its attendant adverb to understand how something is said, it's too late. This is why it makes sense to attribute dialogue close to the start of an utterance, or not at all.

178 | *GLITTERING, SNIGGERING, SMIRK, SLIGHT, quickly.* I have no time for these words in fiction. I appear to despise the letter *i*. What did the *i* ever do to me? (An undergraduate once told me that they hated first-person narrators because they thought, looking at a page, *The only I is me.*) People are always doing things quickly for no reason in fiction. They cross rooms quickly. They drink glasses of water quickly. They glance quickly though there is no other way to glance.

Some writers repudiate all adverbs, for no good reason. It's one of the most common pieces of advice, but I believe the adverb is the most maligned and misused part of speech. (*The* adverb? All adverbs.) People use them unthinkingly. (*Unthinkingly* is an adverb; it adds meaning to the verb it modifies that could not be gotten any other way.) They use them to modify verbs of attribution.

"I love you," she said tenderly.

Pointless. But:

"I love you," she said furiously.

Or:

"I love you," she said doubtfully.

Adverbs are most useful when they contradict what they modify, dialogue or verb or adjective. You might not need an adverb at all: a gesture might do.

"I love you." She cut into her cauliflower as though it took effort.

179 | PEOPLE USE ADVERBS TO EQUIVOCATE. *Slightly, nearly, imperceptibly, almost, kind of, sort of, somehow, perhaps*. Sometimes they double up: *nearly imperceptibly*. Linguistic equivocation is irresistible, but you should resist it, even that namby-pamby verb of beauty, *seems*.

Think of Hamlet: "Seems, madam? Nay, it is; I know not 'seems.'" Tell us not what things might be nor almost do, but what they are.

Oh, how my students love *somehow*, its gauzy magic. Me, too.

Any rule I pass along to fiction writers, I break when I offer it. I am absolute in my beliefs, but I try to ameliorate them with *perhaps* and *I think* and *in my opinion*.

180 A TEACHER ONCE TOLD MY WRITING CLASS, "I don't like sentences that begin, for instance, 'Sitting in traffic on the highway, he pondered his life.'" Somebody asked him why. "It just doesn't sound right," he said, or so I remember. I agree with him—not about his explanation, but I, too, dislike the persistent turning of verbs into adverbs. In my former teacher's example, *sitting in traffic* is an adverb that modifies *pondered*. With any kind of introductory dependent clause like this, you can't understand the sentence until you get to the main verb. I don't mean to get all Strunk and White, talking grammar and style—I don't believe in a single good style—but weakened verbs in fiction drive me around the bend. (What bend? A rhetorical bend.) Better:

> He sat in traffic and pondered his life.

Worse is when verbs are turned into adverbs and characters are run through impossible obstacle courses:

Walking across the room, he sharpened his pencil and called for his mother.

That adverbial *walking* modifies *sharpened* and means the two things happen simultaneously. This seems unlikely, though it's not as bad as the ventriloquial:

"You look wonderful!" she said, drinking her martini.

181 | I CAN'T EXPLAIN WHY I HATE *SNIGGERING* AND *smirk* so much, unless it's because my undergraduate students—my beloved undergraduate students—love and misuse them. There is something unpleasant about people who snigger and smirk, in my opinion, and the dictionary agrees with me, but my students don't: they allow perfectly lovable characters to snigger and smirk.

If a number of young people all have the same misconception about a word, then the meaning of the word will change. It's exciting when language changes, when we're here to see it and are aware. I believe this and even remember, most of the time.

182 | I USED TO CORRECT *ALRIGHT* TO *ALL RIGHT* until *alright* wormed its way into the dictionary. After that I found it aesthetically unpleasing. I still hate *gift* as a verb where *give* will do and sometimes write, in the margin, a crude **No.** I have despised the use of *transpire* to mean

happen instead of, properly, *came to be known*, ever since my father explained it to me. The beauty of the etymology, trans spire, *breathe across*, and the usefulness of this now-lost meaning makes me melancholy. But I don't correct it.

183 DO I HAVE ANYTHING ELSE, IN THE END, TO SAY about language? Yes. Don't attenuate your verbs (she started to, they tried to, he thought about starting to try to). All good language is economical; that is, it doesn't spend more than it needs to achieve the desired effect—but that effect might be extravagance, or mystery; it might be the creation of a human voice that is charming but dishonest, with a black soul and a beating heart. I once did an event with another writer who said that when she edits she goes over and over her language to see if she can make it plainer, clearer, more direct. I laughed and said I went over my language to make it skewed, odder, more beautiful. We were both right.

I tell a lie, as the English say. (Jauntier, funnier, than *I lie* or *I'm lying*.) I don't labor over language, as many excellent writers do. They can spend days on a single paragraph. A single sentence. They deliberate. They put words in and take them out. One comma is cause for intense rumination.

If I don't get a sentence close to right the first time, I know the sentence is wrong. I toss it out or I keep going, but I don't linger. I edit, all the time and in different ways and unsentimentally. When it comes to revision, I cut amounts that would hobble a different writer, or so I tell myself. The idea of spending hours perfecting a single sentence makes my brain hurt, like repeating a word until it no longer sounds like a word.

Perhaps I'm not that interested in The Sentence as a unit of writing, instead preferring turns of phrase on one side and paragraphs on the other. A turn of phrase—an image, a metaphor, a joke—I can type out and think, *Yes, that's good, that's a dopamine hit, no need to stop.* If I'm writing paragraphs I'm moving forward. Even the indentation of each paragraph catapults me ahead. I don't think I'm capable of writing anything that has momentum—that thing that prods or pulls the reader along—unless I feel momentum in the writing.

When I compose I'm a shark. If I stop I'll die.

184 IT'S POSSIBLE THAT I HAVE CUT MORE WORDS FROM my work than I've published. Probable. If I include unpublished books—cutting on a grand scale!—certainly. This used to depress me, but now I consider it part of my panache.

185 KNOWING THAT I'M ALWAYS GOING TO NEED multiple drafts of anything makes me freer in composition, but I still can't bear to write prose that seems incorrect to me, sloppy or dull or flat. I use language to look at the world of my work, to understand every other aspect. I indulge myself. Later I can cut, but at first I can show off.

Is language the most important thing to me, or only the thing I'm vainest about?

Improvisation, again. When I follow language and use it to understand character; when I listen for consequence, let one thing lead to another; when I allow dialogue to do its work—revelation, tussle, slow dance, battle—that's the work that means the most to me. If I think, *Now, where did that come from?* I know something's going right. The work I write with this level of freedom is easier to revise. Flexible, pliant. It doesn't seize up like concrete or dry out like paint.

It's also more likely to be a joyful experience. There's a lot about writing that's difficult or dispiriting. Career and publication and the process itself, as you try to get things right, get closer to the emotional truth of your work, attain your ambitions. You might have a good writing day only to have nightmares from stirring up the fearsome things that had previously settled on the ocean floor of your brain. You might be struck with the belief that you're the worst writer in the world, talentless, with only enough literary sense to understand how short you've fallen. You might be similarly struck with the belief that you're one of the best writers alive and have never gotten your due and perhaps never will.

Take pleasure where you can. Show off. Make yourself laugh.

186 | IF YOUR PARENTS DON'T UNDERSTAND YOUR work, if they don't support or read it: I'm so sorry. And congratulations: you're free. Parental indifference is a great gift for a writer. You can't buy that kind of privacy.

187 NEARLY ANYTHING IS TRAINING FOR WRITING fiction: the good teachers, the bad ones, the playground at an English school with high prison-like walls that block children from view of the outside world, the playground at an American school with cyclone fences all around, easy to hop, a phrase I love, *hop a fence*. (I have never hopped a fence.) I'm married to an Englishman who can't bear the ugliness of cyclone fences—also called chain-link fences, but I prefer *cyclone*, which I assume describes what lengths of fencing look like when rolled up. They are ugly, but they cut everything into diamonds. You can fit a toe through them; you can lace your fingers through; they chime when shaken. They can snag like sweaters. They are a homely material in a beautiful pattern: fiction.

I've now looked it up. They're called cyclone fences because they can stand up to cyclones—the wind blows through the diamonds, making a cyclone fence stronger than a more fortified barrier. This is a pretty good metaphor for nearly anything writing related—if you collaborate with even the most punishing winds, you will withstand anything.

Prose needs some air. The sensibilities of your readers need to flow through. If your work is impenetrable, it will not hold up.

188 SOME PEOPLE MOSTLY THINK IN FIGURATIVE language, some not at all. There are no advanced techniques in fiction, things that you should build up to slowly. Or, there are, but they differ from writer to writer. Meta-

phor may not come easily to you, in which case I would suggest writing a lot of metaphors until you're better at them. Unless you abhor them, in which case, leave them alone.

For me as a reader, figurative language probably gives me greater and more reliable pleasure than anything else, particularly figurative language that also develops character, or gives me a way to see something otherwise indefinable. I never think: oh, what excellent figurative language; it's just that if I have been moved by a sentence or have marveled at it or even felt a quick shock of jealousy, it is some sort of metaphor. This feels neurological, not analytical.

189 | THE WRITING OF METAPHORS SHOULD NOT BE labored, nor automatic. Many a leafless tree has been described as having branches like an old man's hands, reaching for the sky, but do they really? Must all lawns in suburbia be manicured?

190 | ALL FICTION IS A BODY OF WATER: LANGUAGE IS the surface. Some language you pass through instantly: from the first sentence you can see all the way to the bottom. Other language has a higher surface tension—difficulty, eccentricity—and offers resistance. It might confuse a reader at first. Then it teaches you how to read it and you fall in, and the language is something you swim through that shows you the world of the book.

If you change the rules—if you suddenly start spelling dialogue phonetically partway through—your readers are yanked back up to the surface of the water. They're not in it any longer. You can do this on purpose, of course.

191 ALL FICTION MUST TEACH READERS HOW TO read it.

192 SOMETIMES IN CLASS I POINT OUT A WRITER'S favorite word. Then I say, "You're not allowed to use that word anymore," just to see them wince. Often the words have to do with scale—*tiny*, *little*, *enormous*, *vast*—or light—*pale*, *dark*. "At least do a search," I say, relenting, "so you can choose the indispensable instances."

193 *TENDERLY, TENDERNESS, TENDER, PALE, sometimes, vast, perhaps, bespoke, assiduous, autonomic, seize, joy, terrible, awful, disaster, catastrophe, beloved, probably, mostly, eponymous, particular, beauty, beautiful, pleasure, pleasurable, pleasant, thrill, burn*. For this book, in addition, *above all, blockheaded, comfort, by which I mean, that is, this is, bitter, delusion, hubris, in other words, stymie, by the way, ineffable.*

IX

194 | AM I WRITING A CRAFT BOOK? DO I BELIEVE IN craft? Are all these things just made-up notions?

Yes, and yet I love to discuss them with students and argue about them with friends. Writing may feel like an enchantment, but, away from my work, the enchantment can feel too general. I want to examine every part of the spell, to concentrate on the little birds who hold my gown aloft and the mice who adjust my slippers, to the sound of first the forest—the amalgamation—then to each instrument inside, howl (animal or wind), whisper (ditto), what is constant and what (chirp, snap, bark) is sudden. A loon is not a heron, and that makes a difference, not just to me, but to the loon, the heron, and the wide world.

195 | A GRADUATE STUDENT ONCE ASKED ME TO DIScuss the difference between atmosphere, mood, and tone. As though they were layers of the earth, distinct in a cross-section map! I didn't know the difference, hadn't really thought about any of it. *Nonsense*, I thought, and then, *How interesting, yes, I have a lot of thoughts*. The words themselves conjured up the thoughts. As soon as you name something, you can know it. Maybe I just mean I'm coming around to craft.

"Tone," I said to the student, "is the spiritual life of vocabulary and sentence structure." I only remember this because I wrote it down.

Atmosphere, mood, tone, three different terms for how a story can make you feel things. Now I can see them in their multicolor layers, tone closest to the surface of the earth, all three part of the aerosphere, distinct from content. *The horse kicked the boy* is different from, *In the afternoon the horse, for reasons we now know, snorted, and stretched, and drove his hoof at the shoulder of the sullen five-year-old in the corner of the paddock.*

196 IN FICTION—IN ALL WRITING—OPPOSITES WORK together to deepen what's there. Humor amplifies what's sad in fiction and in life; sadness can make jokes funnier. Humor is oxygen in an airless room, allows you to breathe enough to see what's all around you. You don't need laugh-out-loud jokes, just a sense of the absurd, the surreal, the ridiculous. Humor is light. In total blackness, you can't see anything at all, but light throws things into relief. Just a little can do the trick.

197 I DON'T THINK THERE'S ANYTHING YOU CAN'T joke about, though any dark joke should be aimed at your own throat first. If you can take it, so can other people.

198 SOME PEOPLE LOVE ART THAT HAS NO HUMOR TO it. I suspect they are the sorts of people who drink meal replacement shakes and declare them "better than you'd think."

199 I LOVE HUMOR, AS I LOVE ANYTHING OR ANYONE who has saved my life, and if I have a complaint about modern American letters, it's the occasional dismissal of books that are funny. Our puritan forbears: if you enjoy something, it can't be good.

200 OF COURSE I HAVE COMPLAINTS ABOUT MODERN American letters. Come find me at a cocktail party and I'll tell you all of them. When it comes to literature, I'm only in it for the gossip.

201 PERHAPS YOU DON'T LIKE JOKES. LIFE LIKES jokes, is constantly making jokes, even at the most inopportune moments. Probably *particularly* then. In my experience, slapstick and catastrophe live so close together they muck each other up. Tears in the custard pie; custard pie on the gravestone. A lot of young writers are most interested in writing about ineffable sadness. They remove all traces of humor as though with a scalpel, and the patient doesn't survive the surgery.

202 HUMOR IS A KIND OF MEANING. THE AUTHOR MAKES a joke, and the reader finds it funny—and, having done that, the reader knows that there is meaning to be found.

Humor isn't shallow; it's not a glib coping mechanism. It comes from wells inside us as deep as grief and fury and love.

203 JUST BECAUSE SOMETHING'S SERIOUS DOESN'T make it deep.

204 MAYBE ALL THOSE YEARS AGO MY CLASSMATES and I were supposed to avoid specific references to time so we wouldn't write period pieces, work so specific about the current moment it would become nonsensical within the decade. That doesn't happen. Besides, one of the things fiction can do is render a time in all its particularity. Vagueness isn't universal, doesn't radiate down. There's no sunshine without the sun. Only the specific can radiate out into the universe.

Idiosyncratic: one of my favorite things in fiction, one of my favorite words of praise, along with *particular*, *odd*, *strange*, *weird*. Evidence of the world: the loop on a pair of painter's pants, meant to hold a hammer, now ovoid and empty. Canned frosting with a red snap-on lid. A squirrel looking through a glass door like a former tenant. The particular hitching gait of a loved one long dead.

205 | I'M ALWAYS SURPRISED WHEN PEOPLE TELL ME that my most personal and specific work reminds them of their own lives. *But that's* my *mommy*, I want to say, *not yours*.

206 | MICHELANGELO SUPPOSEDLY SAID, WHEN ASKED how to sculpt the *David*, "You take a block of marble and cut away everything that's not the *David*." The sculptor I prefer to think of is Duffy, the Butter Cow Lady of the Iowa State Fair, who sculpted realistic life-sized cows out of tons of butter, veins on udders and tassels on tails. Cows make cream; the dairy makes the butter; the butter lady makes the cow: art. It's possible you could take five tons of butter and cut away everything that's not a cow. Others of us need to churn our own butter. Revision is finding the cow.

207 | I USED TO THINK THAT NOVELS WERE A MORE forgiving form, more capacious. Now I think stories and novels forgive different things. Short stories can be a straight or straightish line or a series of corkscrews or a marble run. They can be mostly plot or absolutely plotless. You can digress, but digression is instantly visible. Short stories are dioramas: they require foreshortening, a moose that's half three-dimensional, half painted on the back wall. Look at that seagull flying over the salt marsh, pure

impressionism. Look at that farmer turning away, because the cranberry bog is what's important and it doesn't matter that the artist isn't good at drawing human faces.

In story drafts, what is often left out is the emotional heart: the writer has hidden it behind a bulkhead of subtlety. It is, as far as I can tell, human nature to dream of subtlety in short stories. Nearly every writer has had the experience of writing a draft of something that feels embarrassingly frank, soppy-sweet, or full of fury, gross, blunt, vulgar, ham-fisted, only to have a reader say, "I don't understand: Do these people like each other?"

Revising short stories is a matter of getting closer and closer to the heart of the matter. There it is, off in the distance, you've walked so far in that direction! Miles and miles over drafts. Dammit, not far enough.

You are inside the story. Inside the house fire. Outside your readers are looking in: they can only see the light; they don't know how you're suffering. You revise to give them some idea.

208 | FOR EVERY POUND OF EMOTIONAL PRESSURE you want your readers to feel, you must apply five hundred pounds on your side of the page. That's just physics.

209 | EVERY GOOD SHORT STORY HAS A BOMB TICKING in its heart. A writer's first instinct will be to defuse it, to

save the characters. It's not your job to defuse it. It's your job to let the bomb go off. That often doesn't happen till the next draft.

210 I USED TO SEND NOVELS CHAPTER BY CHAPTER to my first reader, and she to me. We had an agreement: we would assure each other that we were geniuses; we would say, *Keep going*. If there was a fatal flaw we would reveal it (there never was), and we were available to ask each other questions when we lost faith mid-chapter.

Now I hold on to things much longer. It builds up pressure. I *want* somebody else to read it, because that is how work becomes real. Until then, it's imaginary. I work harder so that I can get somebody else's opinion.

For months or years I write, revise, take notes. I know the world and its people, the flaws and strengths of the book. I am the leading expert, the only expert.

Then somebody—the fellow I'm married to or one of my other early readers—takes it out of my hands and describes it to me. An astonishing feeling. Now it exists. There's more to reckon with. Terrifying, wonderful.

211 YEARS AGO A STUDENT BROUGHT INTO CLASS the brand-new first twelve pages of his novel—the entirety of what he had composed—and I devoted the allotted time to bawling him out for not protecting his work. I did this

because it was such a reckless thing to do, like bringing a newborn baby to a NASCAR race; also, I was killing time so that his classmates wouldn't launch into a critique and ruin it for him. Novels need privacy. They are your dream-world. You may have fallen in love on a first date, but you still shouldn't take that person straightaway to meet your family.

I saw the aforementioned writer recently, twenty-five years later—he's gone on to publish other, different, extraordinary books—and inquired after this novel. "It made a good short story," he told me. It had become real too soon.

212 CAN ANYONE WRITE A NOVEL RIGHT OUT OF THE gate? No, but you can teach yourself if you put your mind to it. The way you teach yourself to write a novel is by writing a novel. No other art form is like this.

Can anyone write a short story? I'm less sure.

213 STORIES YOU CAN HOLD IN YOUR HEAD; NOVELS, unwieldy, you have to trick into holding still in a variety of positions so you can see every angle. When I revise in a computer file I sometimes feel as though I'm working on the façade of an enormous building. How do I get inside? So I print out; I read aloud; I write on enormous pieces of paper pinned to my bookshelves. I outline before the next draft, and write each beat of the novel on a different index

card—*dinner party, exposition about the family's arrival in San Francisco, narrator talks about all the dogs of her life*—until I have a thick stack, a version of my novel I can hold in my hands and rearrange or deal out on my desk and look at all at once; compiling the cards is a helpful form of speed-reading.

I do old-fashioned drafts, a printed copy by my side as I retype the book or the story or the chapter. It's hard not to want to be efficient as a writer, and this sounds like it would take a lot of time, but I've found it the quickest way to get inside of a book. Thorny or abstract problems that have bedeviled me find their solutions; sentences that make no sense refuse to be typed and fall away.

214 WANTING TO BE EFFICIENT IS THE BANE OF FICtion writers, especially novelists. Instinctively you want to swim the English Channel as the crow flies. But there are tides and shallows and occasional pods of jellyfish to take into account. Some obstacles you must go painfully through, and others you must go around or be pulled from, so as not to drown.

In novel writing, as in any endurance sport, the most efficient way is rarely a straight line.

215 IF YOU HAVE A SNEAKING SUSPICION YOU'RE NOT getting some aspect of your novel right—a character isn't clear; your setting doesn't feel palpable—tell yourself you'll

fix it in the next draft. Writing a novel is like carrying a pile of clean laundry in your arms, cumbersome, fragrant, you're impressed with your own efforts. Then you drop a sock. Should you bend down to pick it up? No: you risk dropping your entire armful. You'll remember the sock is there; you can get it later.

That freedom to go on can be useful; it lets you get lost in the world of the book.

Freedom, flexibility, fluidity: a novel needs these. Sometimes a manuscript can seem to stiffen like drying clay, suddenly hard to work with. That can come from thinking you have to get everything right the first time. The trick is to keep it pliable.

216 | NO WRITING IS WASTED. THE DRAWBACK OF NOT being able to think except in typed sentences is that you—I mean *I*—end up with pages and pages of writing that don't go into a book. I keep scrap files on my computer. I console myself by saying those pages are like sketches for a mural, or training for a marathon: the final project could not exist without them.

217 | YOU MAY COME TO BELIEVE, YOU *WILL* COME TO believe, that you can perfect your book, that it has an ideal form that can be found through revision. This is an exalted state, revising to perfect, and a wrongheaded one. If you revise long enough, looking for perfection, which doesn't

exist, and you don't find it, you will despair and adjust and readjust things that seem incorrect, and are by their nature minor.

218 SOMETIMES A WRITER KNOWS ABSOLUTELY EVerything about their characters and writes an entire vivid draft of a novel in which time passes and people die and are born and are changed, and yet there isn't exactly a plot. Such a novel draft is like a chess set, an interesting one, carved and intricate, with the characters where they belong on the board. What isn't yet clear: how each piece moves across, how the characters are introduced to each other, how they interfere with each other—there is no plot without interference—how a move by one affects a move by another. The decisions have been made ahead of time. Half of novel revision is realizing that an insurmountable problem is only insurmountable because of a decision you made six months before. Revising requires new decisions.

There's nothing wrong with this. Every draft gets something else down first. Might be character; might be setting; it might be a compelling, intimate voice. There is no one element a draft needs, and nearly no writer can get it all down at once. It doesn't matter what you begin with, as long as you're willing to look later for what's missing.

219 ONCE IN MY OFFICE I PICKED UP A BOX OF THE index cards I'd post-outlined a novel on to show to a visit-

ing student. I'd bought a handsome cardboard box, mottled like a composition notebook, with a silver pull and frame like a library card catalog drawer. The book was short, and I had shrunk the typeface and printed representative passages out and glued them onto the cards. I was proud of my novel in a box as an artifact; I thought it made me look like a real writer. (Even decades in, I sometimes look for evidence.)

"Look here," I said, and I removed the lid, and there, among the cards, was a lizard. We were in Texas. "Oh! There's a lizard in this box!" I said, and I threw the box if not *at* the student, then not *not* at her, either. The lizard skittered away. We tried to find it so we could escort it into the outdoors, but it had gone behind the bookshelf.

Now I wonder why I was surprised. It seems good, right, that a novel left alone in a box can generate a life of some sort, probably—especially—the sort of life you're not expecting.

X

220 | "WHICH IS YOUR FAVORITE OF YOUR BOOKS? I guess that's like asking which is your favorite child, ha ha ha." Books aren't children, being mostly less interesting and more durable.

Besides, I believe in the evil eye when it comes to both books and children: say as little aloud as possible about their good qualities.

221 | WRITERS IN FICTION WORKSHOPS AND WRITING groups are taught not to take criticism personally, but it's the critics themselves who should not take the stories they read personally. That is, they should not believe that the stories are written for them, their particular interests and ignorance. Read work and meet the work where its intentions lie: that's the only way to be useful as a reader.

No matter what you say about the work, you will be talking to yourself.

My first semester in graduate school, I wrote a patronizing letter for a classmate's minimalist story, concluding, *As you can tell, I don't think less is more. I think more is more.*

What a jerk I was. Miriam, I am sorry.

222 | IN ANY WORKSHOP, EVEN ONE FILLED WITH brilliant, generous readers who are sympathetic to your aims, 20 percent of the advice you will receive will be directly applicable to your work. That 20 percent is gold. There's no substitute for it. The other 80 percent might be well-meaning, well-argued, intelligent—it will just be the critic talking to themself.

It's important, freeing, to remember this, both as critic and as critiqued.

If you revise trying to answer every objection anyone has to your work, you will write something unobjectionable. Nothing is worse than unobjectionable fiction.

223 | THERE ARE SOME THINGS IN A FICTION CLASS that people will say aloud, thinking that the writer has more work to do, when really all they're doing is describing the reader's work. *I didn't know what to think. I didn't know how to take it.* Or else they'll complain about not understanding something immediately, even though, outside of workshop, they know that not understanding something immediately is the point.

224 | THE LAST THING WE WERE TOLD IN GRADUATE school—by classmates, not by teachers—is that the world of publication was so crushing and cruel, so filled with rejection and heartbreak, that the best thing a writing class could do was give you a taste of that misery in the classroom. Toughen you up.

Years later I would read about Tough Mudders, races where people pay money to crawl though trenches and scramble through razor wire and get shocked by live wires and at the end get a medal, and I thought about some of my Iowa classmates. A writing workshop, in my opinion, is where you shouldn't be shocked by live wires for no reason. Nobody needs to be trained to suffer. You need to learn how to dare. Rejection for the best work you can do will still crush you, but at least it will be for work you believe in.

225 WHEN I TEACH, WHETHER I LIKE STUDENT WORK is beside the point. I don't engage the part of my brain that likes or dislikes things globally. Liking, I think, is a binary proposition, and I'm after something more complicated. My job is to work to see what a writer is trying to do, to perceive their highest ambitions (even if they themselves cannot see them), and then to give advice accordingly. Mostly I try to describe both my experience of reading the book, and the book itself: its shape, its themes, its aspirations. When you describe something, it's easier to understand; when you understand something, it's easier to like; and as a result I like most of the work I read as a teacher, though some work strikes me as further away from a writer's aims, some closer. I read to find what's exciting in the work. There is always something.

My own aims in writing are irrelevant. I don't want to teach people to write fiction like mine. Impossible: as I have said before, when I'm writing well I have no idea what

I'm doing. But I'm careful and clear-eyed when it comes to reading other people's fiction. That's what I'm qualified to do. Reading student work is my favorite part of teaching, looking for intention, oddities, foibles, where the writer is taking pleasure and where being merely dutiful. As a reader I want books I've never read before. I go into manuscripts with the same wish.

226 IF, IN THE CLASSROOM, I AM KNOWN TO *LIKE* OR *dislike* things, then students might try to write things to elicit the former and avoid the latter—or to write something that runs against my tastes to teach me a lesson. Some probably do anyhow. They believe (they may be right) that despite everything it's clear what I prefer. I insist that my taste is irrelevant. This means that teaching has broadened my taste immensely, and I now like, admire, understand, love, am moved by, even seek out a much wider variety of fiction than I would have, given my own proclivities—one of many improvements teaching has made upon my personality and habits.

227 WHEN I READ FICTION OFF THE CLOCK, I INdulge in dislike. I'd rather read work that I love, of course, but sometimes I take great pleasure in hating somebody else's work: overrated, unoriginal, slack. I wield a phantom red pen—*This adverb adds no meaning, this is a cliché, you have already used this word six times, who cares, who cares, who cares.*

228 | OVER YEARS I'VE LEARNED NOT TO PANIC IF I read an early draft of a novel by a student that's a mess, as long as the writer is invested in it. I don't even tell them it's a mess: either they know or the tight-rope act that is a novel draft requires that they don't look down and see the disorder. When people bring me partial manuscripts I give very little advice on the work itself, just description, what I find especially fine or exciting or original, and some thoughts on process. Then I say, *Keep going. You have to keep writing.*

Describing a book to somebody is a little—I imagine—like telling their fortune, except with no undercurrent of chicanery or incense. A look passes over the writer's face: *Is that true? I hope that's true.* Some of it is true now, and some exists only in implication but can be made manifest with work. The writer, if interested, can make it true.

(Apologies to my fellow fiction writers who like tarot and astrology. There is, I find, significant overlap in the lovers of tarot and the lovers of karaoke.)

229 | IN MY TEACHING LIFE, I HAVE HAD STUDENTS who have been writing since grade school and came straight out of undergrad, or soon afterward, and others who had whole careers before they applied themselves to fiction. Of the older students, some had put aside dreams of writing for years to raise children or go to law school or work in kitchens or work construction; others recently thought, *You know what? I'd like to write.*

Within a couple of years everyone's level.

It doesn't matter when you start. It only matters that you learn to work, whatever that looks like. If you are a middle-aged beginner, you can catch up very quickly to the youngsters. Everything you have done in your life before you start writing, good habits and bad behavior, is preparation for fiction writing. Those years will save you time.

230 | PROGRESS IN WRITING IS NEVER A STRAIGHT line: you can know something a long time, years even, before you can deploy it. You get better not by steady evolution but by spontaneous generation. Previously your stories (according to readers) has been tentative and obscure. You agree. You write another. Still tentative, still obscure.

Then all at once, in the next story, everything you know *works*. Characters act, language illuminates. Not just that: your own understanding of what fiction can do seems to have expanded geometrically.

That's been my experience watching students. My own experience, too. The first decent short stories I wrote were out of order, overfilled, overpopulated, reckless, a huge improvement on the careful intellectual stories I'd been writing. (I never revised those older stories. I couldn't imagine making them better: they had achieved their small ambitions.)

231 | THE CURE FOR ALL WRITERLY MALADIES IS work. This is particularly true for jealousy over somebody else's work or career. If you are feeling competitive with

somebody else's writing, take that energy and go to your desk. If you are worried about what will happen to your work when you've finished it, dive into work. If you wonder what it's all for, work. If reading these words makes you irritated, or you want to explain to me how it's not that easy, I understand. Take that irritation and write a paragraph.

232 | FICTION NEEDN'T BE MANNERLY OR APPROPRIATE. It can be offensive, as life is offensive—though offensiveness itself is a low ambition.

233 | IF YOU ARE AT HEART A COMPETITIVE PERSON, AS some writers are, lose as quickly as you can the habit of comparison. Decide that you are in a category of one. It's hard to do, especially when the publishing world specifically asks for that terrible parlor game, *comps*, books you think are like your own work, but living without comparing yourself to other writers is a holy state of ignorance. It doesn't have to be an act of modesty but of quiet grandiosity.

I'm not perfect at it, but I get better every day.

234 | DECADES AGO I DECIDED THAT, AS MUCH AS I could, I would not learn the quantitative measures of another writer's career, not advances nor sales figures. I knew I would never do anything good with the knowledge; I would feel jealous or pitying. (Once I learned that a writer

I greatly respected had sold fewer than three hundred copies of his well-reviewed book. It was like seeing a picture of him in his underpants.) Often those numbers mean nothing. So many measures of success in fiction don't really measure success: an enormous advance that never comes close to earning out and hobbles a young writer's career; a book that sells a lot of copies followed by one that doesn't. It's difficult not to dream when you send work into the world, but try not to dream quantitatively. We're not in it for the numbers.

235 DO I OCCASIONALLY FEEL SOMETHING ABOUT the success of another writer? I'm not a saint. It does happen. If the other writer is a good person and a good writer, I don't resent them. The same for a good writer and a bad person. A good person and a bad writer—this is the most difficult scenario for me, but no.

A bad writer and a bad person—yes, and then I am always relieved to discover that anyone I trust also dislikes both author and work.

236 I KNOW SEVERAL WRITERS WHO HAVE RUINED their careers with jealousy. They'd already decided that what they were interested in was publishing success. Several of them attained it. But then a book didn't do as well as expected, or the next book didn't sell.

The only thing to do, ever, is write the next book. These writers did. But not their own books, not the books of their hearts. They got obsessed with books that had done better than theirs, and they wrote to what they thought was the market, books they didn't believe in.

They became that most awful thing: writers who resent any other writer at all.

Not coincidentally, these are people who'd been told while they were young, in graduate school, that they were going to be the Next Big Thing. Except there is no Next Big Thing in fiction, or if there is, you wouldn't want to be it. It's not a lifetime appointment.

237 | JEALOUSY IS NORMAL AND USUAL, BUT I AM JUST old-fashioned enough to believe in repressing certain normal and usual emotions. No, not repressing: repurposing. Grief you should give in to, and everyone needs to know how to express anger, but jealousy over somebody else's career or work gets you nowhere. Worse, it's one of those habits that produces so much heat and feeling, once you start it's hard to stop, like compulsive handwashing, or licking your lips: it is the licking that causes the burning, but all you can think is that it must also be the cure.

238 | BEFORE THE PUBLICATION OF A BOOK, FOR TWO or three or fourteen nights, I worry about bad reviews.

Sometimes I take to my bed and stare at the ceiling. I'm not afraid of being misunderstood: I'm afraid of humiliation. Then the feeling passes. Like most things, actual bad reviews aren't nearly as terrible as the threat of them (though I have flung a few drinks in a few faces, in my imagination).

239 | IF YOU'RE DOING IT RIGHT, JUST BEFORE YOUR first publication, you will be overcome with terror. You are about to be exposed: people will know things about you, your parents will guess that you've had sex. You only have to cross this river once. The next time you'll be blasé about what you've accidentally or purposefully revealed.

240 | CONFIDENCE ISN'T A REQUIREMENT FOR WRITers, but try to cultivate it anyhow, even if only at your desk, all by yourself. You needn't cloak it in self-deprecation, either. I am a habitual self-deprecator and must remind myself that it can be off-putting; it often puts me off in others.

There is no writer viler than somebody who, upon being congratulated for an honor, instead of saying thank you, says, "I think it must be a mistake." Or, "I don't know what they were thinking." Or insists that an objectively wonderful award "humbles" them. I don't trust any writer who doesn't know the meaning of the word *humble*.

241 WHEN IT COMES TO PUBLISHING, STRIVE FOR very low expectations. *No* expectations would be ideal, but that's impossible, a don't-think-of-a-hippopotamus sort of thing. Low, existing in relation to other points on the graph, gives you a visual, is achievable. You don't want to have nice things happen to you and your book and end up miserable, because your wildest dreams—or the wildest dreams of your agent—didn't come true.

242 LIKE ANYTHING THAT IS BOUGHT AND SOLD, fiction is subject to fashion, and nowhere is that as evident as in titles. *The Farrier's Daughter*, *The Pharmacist's Wife*; *What We Cannot Know*, *Look for Me Later*, *What the Dark Reveals*; *The Unfathomables*, *The Insufferables*; *Bright Animals*, *Big Americans*; *An Unholy Woman*. None of these are bad titles, and some of the original versions are even beautiful, but titles that resemble other titles are hard to remember. Perhaps my library training prejudices me: every librarian or bookseller has tried to help a person who says, "I can't remember the title, but it has 'girl' in it." That might be enough to find a book the month of publication, but it gets more difficult the older the book. A book title is, in a way, an advertisement.

Short story titles are different: they are closer to first lines, and can be willfully gorgeous, even obscure.

As a teacher I believe myself to be generous and open-minded, except when it comes to titles, when I am an absolute opinionated jerk. I revel in it. "Don't like it," I'll say. Or, "That sounds like a gift shop in an airport." Some of my fondest conversations I have with former students are about now published, successful work with titles I was rude about. The bad titles didn't hurt the books. I still think they're bad titles.

I like a title with sonic pleasure, at least one arresting word. It's nice when an image is called up. I like to fiddle with articles, taking them on and off. I think pronouns are too common in titles (my first book has a two-pronoun title); I think it should only be a title for your book (I have two books with titles previously claimed by others). With my three short story collections, I had the title for the book before I knew which story would receive it; I don't know why. My first two novels I stubbornly titled myself; my third I changed my mind halfway through; my fourth had an anodyne title I was attached to and then my editor suggested a much better one, and I forget it was ever called anything else.

I'm not sure how I feel about the title of this book.

243 | WHAT I WROTE ON THAT PEPTO-BISMOL BOX AT the jazz club was a list of titles for this book, stolen from songs. *Almost Like Being in Love: Notes on Fiction.* Or, *The Very Thought of You: Notes on Fiction. The Long and Winding Road: Notes on Fiction. You're Nobody Till Somebody Loves You: Notes on Fiction.*

244 ANY JOB THAT ALLOWS YOU TO DAYDREAM IS good for a writer. I worked in the same public library from the time I was fifteen until I was twenty-two, first shelving books, then behind the circulation desk. On weekends I arrived early to turn on the computer, a process that in those days took half an hour. I knew when I finished my graduate program in writing that I would go to library school, because I had a sense that I needed a steady job that had nothing to do with writing and didn't require a driver's license, which I didn't then have.

I recommend jobs that you think you could do forever. They don't need to be completely fulfilling. Ideal for them to be at least minorly fulfilling, or to give you a different sort of meaning than your writing. I loved library work because all day long people asked me questions that I could answer; I did; they were largely grateful. It was mostly not work that I took home or worried about at night, though day by day I cared about it a lot.

245 IT'S DANGEROUS FOR A PERSON WHO REALLY wants to write to also care about having a job that sounds like a job a writer should have: teaching too many courses at too many schools; writing grants or advertising copy; working in publishing. Not impossible; some people manage it, and advertising particularly seems like good training for making up things linguistically. Still, over the years I've known a lot of people who can't divide their ambitions

and imaginations into useful portions. They get a job; they give up writing.

This includes people with really good teaching jobs, with reasonable course loads and tenure, a life of the mind, summers off. Such a teaching job (I have such a teaching job) is seen as a sign of success for a writer. Nearly any job will fill up any time you allow; academia away from the students involves a lot of busywork and hand-wringing.

Don't teach if you don't love teaching. It will be wretched for everyone involved.

If you do love teaching, you must be careful not to give up the long-term gratification of writing for the short-term gratitude of colleagues and students.

246 | AS A TEACHER, I HAVE INSTALLED MOATS around my writing time. Some of my colleagues—especially the every-day writers—read student work all year round. I do not. I protect my writing time and my writing and also my beloved students. By saying no I am protecting them from my resentment and also, I hope, being a good role model. I also don't read work for people once they've graduated. No to everything and everyone, so I don't have to think about it, the way, as a circulation librarian, I required ID from anyone who didn't have a library card, teenagers and senior citizens, those dressed in suits or off-color T-shirts. Even a nun, once, which shocked my staff. Every now and then somebody asks me to read something in my writing time and it's a worthy project and I'm fond of the

student and I almost bend. Then I picture the fortified wall of my moat cracking, springing a leak.

No.

247 | YOU WILL KNOW THAT YOU'RE DONE WITH something when you can't imagine making it better. For some writers that's a state of exhilaration: They've done everything they can. This beautiful accomplishment! Nothing can improve it. Others of us arrive at the same place, despondent: This ramshackle thing. I've reached the end of my powers. Nothing can improve it.

248 | MORE THAN ONCE A GRADUATE STUDENT HAS come to me with a novel they've been working on for years. They're on the second draft, or the fifth. It's become a battle: they're punch drunk. Without exception these students are hardworking and ambitious—they already know it's a long game—but they're no longer sure of the book at hand. They wonder if they should give up.

"Let me read it," I say.

Sometimes it's only that the writer has lost sight of the book, as though it's an enormous, fully formed garment that they've gotten turned around in. They've been resolutely jamming their head in one of the sleeves, have got one arm stuck in the lining, and the pockets are still stitched shut by the haberdasher. In conversation we can get it turned around. I might tell them to put the book in chronological order. "It sounds like a lot of work," I say, "but you can do it in a week." Or it's even quicker, a matter of cutting the first two chapters.

Other times, I read and can see that the writer's relationship to the material is habitual, not emotional. They know more now. They chose material they thought they were capable of writing about and now they're a different, better writer. The book may not be dead, but it's sound asleep. Should they wake it up? Maybe I'll say, "You know, it's pretty good!" Chances are the book *is* pretty good, but no more than that.

Sometimes it's my job to say, "I think it's time to stop working on this book. You don't love it anymore." I talk about the books, four of them, that I myself have walked away from. (It might be five; I have a draft of a novel that I'm wavering about.)

I say this only to students who I believe are ready to hear it. I say it gently, and with genuine excitement about the future. "You're tough," I tell them (which is what I tell myself). "Sure, it hurts. You can take it. No writing is wasted. You needed to write this, but now you need to write something else, the book beyond this book. Tell me what you think that might be. Tell me about *that* book."

So far that next book has always been astonishing.

249 IT ISN'T REALLY TOUGHNESS YOU NEED. THAT'S my mother's word (my mother was pretty tough). A writer needs to be resilient. To bend when something might break

you; to understand that rewards—advances got, copies sold, bookstores read at—can come and go, and they aren't actually a comment on your work and they're certainly not a comment on you yourself. When I despair or doubt, I tell myself that I am an artist. That is both highfalutin and modest: it gains me nothing. It promises nothing. But it puts me back inside me, where art occurs, and nothing is quantifiable.

250 | NO CAREER INCLINES ONLY UPWARD. FAILURE follows success; success can come again. The book you're working on might not get published, so you better try to like what you write. The only thing worse than writing a book you believe in that you can't publish is writing one you don't believe in and can't publish—though writing a book you don't believe in and publishing it sounds rotten to me. Might do damage to your career, to your understanding of yourself.

251 | HARD NOT TO THINK THERE'S A FUTURE IN which your career will be different—when the things you've longed for are in your lap—and you can rest. No writer ever stops thinking this, not even the very successful ones. The lucky break. It's why people buy lottery tickets.

Your writing life is right now, whatever that looks like. It is already underway. Don't wait to write the work you've always wanted to. Don't put things off, waiting for luck to change your life and career. Arrange your life now to be as conducive to writing as it can be.

252 WHEN MY KIDS WERE YOUNG I READ ARTICLES about parenting. I came across a study that said parents should never tell their children that they're smart or talented. Intelligence and talent are static characteristics that reside inside the person, and a child who is told they're talented and smart might worry that at any moment they could disprove it: they're ordinary, everyday chowderheads. Working hard, on the other hand, is an action, visible, something any child, or writer, can do. Praising the result of hard work will inspire a child to keep working.

There are writers in workshops who, everyone agrees, are *talented*. When people speak of talent in this way, they nearly always mean language: the writer is doing something unusual and moving and beautiful with grammar and word choice and figurative language and punctuation. *Talent* almost never refers to an understanding of plot; people think the damnedest things about plot, me included. We think of plot and setting as belonging to the story, and I think that's right; we speak of language as belonging to the writer, and I think that's wrong. Several of my students who were particularly invested in language stopped writing once they graduated, or even before. It breaks my heart. As I saw it happening, I tried to intervene. I was kind and I flattered. I was mean and I hectored. I asked what they thought might help. Sometimes you have to put the fear of God into a person. You can only hope they're more afraid of God than of failure.

253 | I DON'T TELL MY STUDENTS THAT THEY'RE TALented any longer. Now I try to see what a writer is interested in, not what I think they're good at.

254 | LUCKILY, AN APPETITE FOR WORK IS THE MOST essential quality in a writer, and it's something you can, with some effort, acquire: I am living proof. I do sometimes tell ghost stories, the ghosts being former students and classmates who never learned how to work, who excoriated themselves over their writing instead of over their work habits.

Talent, if it's a thing that exists, and I'm not sure it is, is static, internal, never enough. Part of your inner life. Your Neverland. It must be unnerving to hear it described, reduced to one word, something that people believe in or, worse, don't.

255 | NOTHING PERFECT IS INTERESTING. SOMETIMES a student who is struggling to get work to me will say, "My problem is that I'm a perfectionist." I always answer, "Oh, you don't like to fail in public, unlike the rest of us?"

"No, no," they say. "The problem is I'm my own harshest critic."

"If that were really true," I say, "then you would have no trouble at all with showing me work."

I'm a perfectionist. They say it apologetically and boastfully, a character flaw that speaks of high standards. Not *I'm better than you*, but *I need to be better than you*. Nobody ever modestly said they were a perfectionist.

256 | SOMETIMES I THINK I'D LIKE TO HAVE AN ADVICE column, then I realize my answer to every single letter would be, "Buck up, for God's sake." I don't believe that bucking up is the answer to every problem, just that bucking up never hurt. *Bucking up* is not the same thing as *sucking it up*. Bucking up is not an endpoint: once you've done it, you can go on to other things.

257 | IT IS THE FLAWED, THE ODDBALL, THE BROKEN, that is magnificent. The perfect doesn't interest me. It has no personality.

258 | IF YOU'RE NOT AFRAID OF FAILING AS A WRITER, it means you haven't risked enough. Or you might be a sociopath. There are some good writers who are sociopaths.

259 | NO: IT'S TERRIBLE TO TELL WRITERS THAT THEY'RE talented, or due success. Good work will eventually be rewarded, but it can take years, and if you've been led to believe it will be easy you're more likely to give up. Nobody actually knows what book will be a great success, not agents or publishers; they only know what was successful last year.

260 | I FINISHED WRITING MY FIRST BOOK IN 1991. BEFORE it was published two years later, I came to believe—a kind of religious belief—that it was abysmal, both plagiarized and also my own rotten original work, with characters whose inner and outer selves were made of saltines, nothing at stake, leaden prose, dull, dead. Projected upon the screen of my brain was my book's actual form, it felt like, suddenly visible.

The book's publication was quiet. A few months before, the imprint that bought it was shuttered, all the editors fired. My agent suggested that I go to New York to meet the editor at the publishing house who'd inherited the collection. Just as I walked into her office, the fax of my first review ever came in. "I think there's some stuff we can use in here," said my new editor, and I sat and read the review on its curling thermal paper, which I had to unroll like a proclamation. It called my stories "well-crafted but dispassionate and cheerless."

I left the office and hurried into the nearest bar, which turned out to be a TGI Fridays. Later, I found myself in a salsa club. We'll speak no more of it.

261 EVENTUALLY I PUBLISHED A SECOND BOOK, AND a third. The hatred I felt for them just before publication eclipsed the hatred I felt for that first book. Soon enough I began to think sentimentally of my first collection. It was the best I could have written at the time. Juvenilia. No point in wishing it better: I'd done what I could.

262 DON'T GET ME WRONG: FOR EVERY DEPTH OF DESPAIR, I feel its opposite at some point. I keep it to myself.

263 IF YOU HAVE SOME SUCCESS IN YOUR WRITING life, through luck and hard work, remember that private pleasure in success is just as sweet as that which you shout from the rooftops. Sweeter, sometimes. You don't have to feign modesty. You can exult. Tell a nonwriter beloved. You can have a ritual little dance of happiness.

264 THE EDITOR WHO'D BOUGHT MY FIRST COLLECTION ended up back at the same publishing house, published my second and third books, then gave me a contract for a fourth. We went through years of revision and multiple drafts. Then she decided not to publish it. She had her assistant call with the news. Nothing in my life, including the most poisonous comments scrawled by the worst old classmate, could have prepared me.

I spent twenty-four hours as a weeping, moaning wretch. I lived in Paris then, in a literal garret. My husband was traveling. I remember every posture I assumed, alone in that picturesque apartment, either end of the sofa, all the angles of the bed, the dining room chairs, the slipper bathtub. The next day I asked my agent, "If I revise this book, do you think it will be a great book, or just a good book?" After a pause he said, "A good book."

"Well, then," I said. "That's that."

Certainty can be a kind of balm. I never want to write a book that's merely good. Aim for great, end up a disaster. I'd rather that.

265 | THE EDITOR DIDN'T CANCEL THE CONTRACT, just kicked the deadline down the road. I started another book, which I worked on for years, through moves and catastrophes and a memoir about the major catastrophe, which the editor didn't want but another editor did. I worked on the novel, drafts and drafts, and then she turned that book down, too. That's the middle unpublished novel, number three. I have never read it again.

266 | I'M TELLING YOU THIS NOT OUT OF FURY OR REVENGE. I loved that editor, who was brilliant and taught me innumerous things about fiction, structure, language, everything. She loved me, too (if not, in the end, my later

work). If it had been a purely business relationship we would have parted much sooner, though it did end amicably, and later she died too young, and I was grief struck, glad that we'd had conversations of sweetness after our professional relationship ended. I will probably puzzle over this time of my writing and publishing life forever.

I spent years of my life working on those two rejected books. Like all important things in my life, at first I was ashamed; then I was at peace; now I'm proud. Part of my bona fides. I'm just that tough.

267 THING IS, I WAS NEVER GOING TO QUIT. THE only thing that makes me feel better after writing breaks my heart is writing.

268 THE ONLY THING THAT MAKES ME FEEL BETTER after anything has broken my heart is writing. This has been true over the decades and through a wide variety of heartaches: the usual dumb ones that I also treat with whiskey and music, sudden grief, expected but wrenching loss, terror about the future (my own, the world's). Yes, there are other, concrete actions to be done, but writing is what allows me to do them, what gets me away from revving the engine while in neutral. It puts me in gear.

If I can write a little, I feel competent. It is one of the few things that makes me feel that way.

269 I MIGHT BE MOST MYSELF WHEN I WRITE; THAT is, I think of no other living human. I worry about nobody's feelings but my own. This isn't the only way to write, but it's the hard-hearted way I do it.

270 I'M FOND OF MOST MY STUDENTS. I'M NOT SURE how I've pulled that off, being intolerant of people generally.

271 SOME DAYS I THINK ANYTHING CAN BE A METAphor for fiction. My favorites, as you may have noticed, involve water—rivers, ponds, pools—ways of moving through or across—boats, submarines, ocean liners. Swimming, always. Diving. Holding your breath. Water at all levels and the kind of greenery that grows at depths and on surfaces. Shipwrecks and crossings. The Winchester Mystery House, a 160-room mansion built by the widow of the heir to the rifle fortune then renovated and added onto for decades, with stairs that lead to ceilings and doors to nowhere and round-the-clock construction that might have been to scare off the ghosts of people killed by Winchester rifles, and might have been because Sarah Winchester herself was a visionary amateur architect with the money to build her visions. Cooking—baking particularly—and painting, both the act and the product. Very rarely, but sometimes, sculpture. Love, always, romantic, parental,

filial, obligatory. Lifting weights. Magic tricks. Dancing. Human anatomy, particularly organs and muscle. Cross sections in children's books. Dolls, both china and rag. As with my fiction itself, some of this is highly autobiographical and some not at all: I swim daily. I love boats but understand nothing of them except how to buy a ticket for the ferry. I lift weights, or have. I don't dance; even my childhood lessons in the Hustle and the Irish Jig have left me. I cannot paint, and in fact was told this in junior high school with fondness by an art teacher, who assured me that I could do other things, like draw. I can't draw. I can follow a recipe but cannot improvise in the kitchen, cannot in fact improvise anything at all, cannot carry a metal tune with magnet mittens, took years of flute—flute! My most hated instrument even before I picked it up!—and was kept in the school band for purely ornamental reasons until I finally quit. I can do nearly nothing off the top of my head except, in a classroom, talk about fiction, but even then somebody has to give me work to read or ask me a question.

272 | I AM TALKING TO MYSELF. *I THINK, I BELIEVE, I imagine, For me.* Copy and paste as many times as you need and scatter throughout this book. I should have rubber stamps made up, packaged with every copy. Sometimes I think I should have rubber stamps made up for my habitual manuscript marginalia, to save time and guarantee legibility: *sounds good, means? Sez who? Eek! All very fine,*

awk., not the right word I don't think, perfect, better? Huh? No., where are they? Where are they? WHERE? lovely, so lovely, this is all so lovely, so good, ✓, ✓! ✓✓.

273 IF YOU HAVE READ THIS BOOK AND THOUGHT, over and over, *That's not for me*. Or, *I wish I could, but that doesn't work for my life*. Or, *What a nice thought if you're lucky*. Or: *Wrong, wrong, wrong, wrong.* Or: *You have left me out, me and my writing and the books I most admire*: I apologize. As a teacher and a writer, I work to be inclusive, but I know I can't be universal. Nothing can be universal without being nonsensical. I wish I could read your work and tell you what I think, which is what I do when I teach. I still might get it wrong, but I would be able to be specific.

274 "WOULD YOU EVER WRITE A MEMOIR?" PEOPLE used to ask me. "God, no," I answered. Autofiction? Never touch the stuff. A craft book? No way. Early on I was certain that I knew the sorts of books I would write for the rest of my life. I didn't understand that each book would change who I was as a writer, even the ones I didn't publish: no writing is wasted.

It's been a joy to write this.

Joy? Yes, I think so. That's what I need to experience for a book to be a book of my heart. I need to write sentences, at least sometimes, that make me think—as I compose them—*Lookit that!*

It's embarrassing to admit; it will disappear soon enough.

275 | OTHER WRITERS GET THEIR THRILLS ELSEwhere. They ski or play video games; they run for the endorphins. They perform karaoke. I teach for the endorphins. If I only wrote, I sometimes think, I would be left with all these questions I couldn't answer. When they show up in other people's work, I can answer them.

When I was younger I would have said that my teaching and writing were absolutely separate. Again, what a jerk I was! Just as there are no prodigies in fiction, there are no masters, no writer whose mastery is so complete that there's nothing else left to learn. Fiction is an art, which means that it changes: inside the writer, and in the world. I don't think I would keep writing if I thought I knew everything there was to know about the practice.

276 | I MEANT TO SAY EVERYTHING I WROTE IN THIS book. I've already changed my mind about some of it.

277 | *NONFINITO* MEANS NOT FINISHED, ART THAT IS rough, on purpose or circumstance. It's a painting that looks like a sketch for another painting—the face rendered but the clothing done in quick brushstrokes, the canvas primed but not filled in. It's a sculpture with one carved

arm rising from the block of marble, alive though rooted in inanimation.

Books on writing must be *nonfinito*. There is no such thing as comprehensiveness. Every writer is different, needs different things at different times, believes different things. I wake up most early mornings these days remembering one more thing I want to get into this book. I imagine this will continue for years after its publication. Perhaps till death, like Sarah Winchester.

What I know this year about writing is different from what I'll know next. It has to be: otherwise my writing would be nothing but pavement, set, unchangeable, this block of sidewalk the same as the next.

Nonfinito is not so far away from the infinite.

278 | IT'S A LONG GAME. THAT'S ALL I EVER WANT TO impart to my students. What matters is that you learn to get work done in the way that is possible for you, through consistency or panic. Through self-recrimination or self-delusion or self-forgiveness: every life needs all three.

279 | WRITERS HAVE EGOS THAT ARE LIKE SOUFFLÉS, enormous and given to collapse. Writing anything and expecting somebody else to read it is an act of hubris, but nothing good can be written without persistent doubts, one of the paradoxes of a writing life. I don't believe that I have ever taught anyone to write. Every writer in the end is

an autodidact. It's a lifelong course of study, or should be. You must believe that you are the only person for this job, which is a fact.

280 | THE FIRST DAY OF WORKSHOP, I TELL MY STUDENTS that a writer has a mantra, and it's the same one for everybody:

I am a genius with much to learn.

INDEX

Numbers refer to subsections.

A

adverbs, 59, 168, 178–180
cutting explanatory (advised), 168
linguistic equivocation and, 179
misused and maligned, 97, 178
turning verbs into (not advised), 180
use/overuse of "quickly," 178
when they are most useful, 178
atmosphere, 195
audience/readers, 14, 160, 207, 208
appearance of text or font and, 165, 167, 169–172
characters and, 57, 69, 131
explanatory conjunctions, adverbs, and, 168
first lines and, 6
gesture and, 138
humor and, 202
lack of control over, 97
language of fiction and, 190
narrators and, 51, 53–55, 57, 63–65, 67, 69
needless mysteries and, 70
preferences of, 70
present tense and, 7
readers for a work in progress, 210, 211, 221–224
realism in fiction and, 128
secrets in fiction and, 153
time in a novel and, 81–85
what interests readers, 19, 100, 106–108
the writer's voice and, 90–91
autobiographical fiction, 114–116, 162, 271

B

bookstores, 117
Boston University Literary Guild, 159
butter cow, Iowa State Fair, analogy for revision, 206

C

chapters, 84, 161
breaks as punctuation, 164, 165
exciting first, mind-numbing second, 84
length, 7, 161, 164

character, 42, 43, 47, 117, 119–123, 125, 127–130, 133–144, 146, 148
accidental patterns and, 117
in autobiographical fiction, 114, 115
bad habits needed by, 120
childhood memories and, 149
clothing and, 144
creation of, 117, 119–123, 185
dialogue and, 175, 176
empathy versus compassion and, 132
failure and, 127
figurative language to develop, 188
in first drafts, 127
gestures and activities for, 138
improvisation, apprehension, and, 119
interiority of, 142, 143
a kink or shameful secret for, 140
language and, 177, 185
letting characters react to facts, 141
McCracken's plots and, 150, 151
minor characters, 58
names for, 128
narrator as a character, 47–49, 51, 53–55, 57–60, 63–67
novels and, 125–126
physical characteristics, 121–123, 139
physicality of, 133–139
plot and, 156, 160
readers knowing more than, 70
setting and, 144–146
short stories and, 124, 125
the subconscious and creating, 117
understanding characters, 57, 58, 119, 130, 131, 142
ways to develop, 120, 121
the writer's own flaws in, 30
writing about people who are demographically different from you, 130, 131
See also narrators
childhood
children as characters, 67, 68
as material for writing, 101, 102
McCracken's memories of outrage and dross, 102
confidence, 44, 240
craft books, 3, 4, 13, 14
advice as inclusive, not universal, 273
different ideas among writers and, 13
how to use the advice in, 9
how to use this book, 12
nonfinito and, 277
technique versus craft, 15
uplifting advice, versus self–loathing, 27
critics and criticism, 221, 222
feedback in workshops, 221, 222, 223
not responding to every objection, 222
"toughening up" a writer, 224
useful percentage of, 222

D

David (sculpture, Michelangelo), 206

diagramming sentences, 61
dialogue, 4, 174–177
as action, 175, 177
gestures and, 178
how McCracken composes, 176
phonetic dialogue, 67
as a problem solver, 175, 176
punctuation for, 176
"said is dead" advice, 177
digression, 12
in short stories, 207
Disney World, 74
rides at, as narrative, 74
doubt, 249
failure versus, 93
McCracken and, 29, 249
drafts, 43, 45
composed on computers, 173
how to keep a manuscript easy to work with, 215, 216
McCracken's drafts for her novels, 162, 213
McCracken's post–draft outlines, 164, 219
multiple drafts as liberating, 185
needs of each draft, 218
a novel draft that is like a chess set, 218
short story drafts, 123, 207
when a writer gets stuck and, 248
writer's relationship to characters in first drafts, 127
Drag Queen Karaoke, Governor Bradford restaurant, Provincetown, Massachusetts, 92

E

ego (of writers), 279
epiphanies, 7
exercises
periodic visualization, 137
a stranger walks into the room (awkwardness exercise), 147
exposition, 71, 73
how to establish the time period, 71
letting the reader interpret, not decode, 71
words versus a camera, 71

F

failure, 93
after success, 250
doubt versus, 93
fear of failure, 258
McCracken's craft talk *On Failure*, 88, 92
as motivation, 93
quivering versus momentum and, 93
wasted worry and, 96
fiction
absolutes as helpful, 7
"ambition is everything," 19
answering the question: "*Can a book . . .*," 162
autobiographical fiction, 114–116, 162, 274
being specific and idiosyncratic, 204
as a body of water: language is the surface, 190
character, 55, 117–148
elements of, 4

fiction (*cont.*)
essentials aspects of, 46
fashions in, 242
first inklings of a piece, 42
first paragraphs, 52
as a fluid substance, 72
how McCracken learned to write fiction, 159
lessons from playwriting, 159
lessons from writing poetry, 160
lessons we must never learn, 40
literary fiction, 8, 100
measures of success in, 235, 236
as a mirror of life, 82
most interesting question in, 152
narrator types, 47–73
needful mysteries and needless mysteries in, 70
the Next Big Thing and, 236
offensiveness in, 232
the ordinary or average in, 140
out-of-the-text writing and, 57
plot, 150–156
readers' interpretations of, 97, 191
"realistic" fiction, 82
the real world and, 62
rules, 7, 17, 18, 21, 179
setting, 145, 146, 204
structure, 162–172
training for writing fiction, 187
as a "trick of the mind," 29
universality and, 52
what it is, 4
why McCracken writes fiction, 41
willingness to make mistakes, 19
See also material; narrative choices; *specific elements*
figurative language, 188
character development and, 188
clichés, 140
McCracken as a reader and, 188
metaphors, 188, 189
first-person narrator. *See* narrators
First Person Singular (book), 48
first sentences, 5, 6, 59, 161, 188
flashbacks, 82–84
footnotes, 162

G

genre, 8, 10, 130, 170
graphic novels, 4
grudges, 22

H

Hamlet (Shakespeare), 179
Hugo, Victor, 35
Hubbard, Mrs. (McCracken's 10th grade English teacher), 61
humble, meaning of, 240
humor, 196–199, 201–203
jokes, 197, 201, 202
as a kind of meaning, 202
McCracken's love of, 199
paired with sadness, 196
slapstick's proximity to catastrophe, 201

I

idiosyncratic, in fiction and as a word of praise, 204
imposter syndrome, 30
interiority (of characters), 142
  common descriptions in works that lack interiority, 143
Iowa Writers' Workshop
  concern with "voice," 90, 91
  McCracken and, 21, 89, 100
  rules for fiction from, 21
  short stories as apprentice work for novels, 124
  the thesaurus, derided at, 11
  "write every day" advice, 23
italics, 171, 172
  overuse of, 171

J

jealousy, 30, 40, 231, 234–237
  a jealous character, 30
  a jealous writer (led to ruin), 236

L

language, 11, 12
  as an element of fiction, 4
  good language as economical, 183
  language centers of characters, 176
  linguistic beauty, 100
  McCracken's dislikes, preferences, 178, 181, 182
  McCracken's interest in, passion for, 15, 44, 89, 91, 183
  meaningless advice and, 21
  as means to enter fiction, 190
  overuse of certain words, 192
  reading aloud and hearing the written word, 89
  rigor and, 91
  talent and, 252–254
  transpire, now-lost meaning, 182
  a turn of phrase, 183
  understanding characters and, 185
  uninteresting, cliché-ridden 140, 141
  verbs as descriptive, 59
  when language changes, 182
  why explanatory conjunctions and adverbs should be cut, 168
  See also adverbs
literary fiction, 8
Lyon, Norma "Duffy," Butter–Cow Lady of the Iowa State Fair, 206

M

mantra for writers, 280
material (what to write about), 98, 100
  autobiographical material, 114–116, 162, 271
  a book of your heart and, 15, 274
  childhood and, 28, 149
  finding the master cylinder, 113
  interesting material, 56, 101
  material for McCracken's early stories versus current work, 102

material (*cont.*)
meaning in, 112
necessity (the thing you must write), 107
objects conjuring up the past, 28
other people's ideas, 103
personal and abstract material, 102, 105
tips for awakening imagination/the subconscious, 117
what's wrong with "write about what you know," 104
a writer's relationship with the material, 100, 101
a writer's soul and, 29
writing about childhood, 101, 102
writing about children, 67, 68
writing about horrible experiences, terrible things, 107, 110
writing about jobs, 106
writing about place/geography, 101
McCracken, Elizabeth
as an aphorist or metaphorist, 15, 271
book reviews and, 238
books she's walked away from, 78, 126, 248
childhood memories, 5, 28, 48, 61, 74, 101,102
clothes worn in high school, 41
early jobs, 33
early realist stories, 160
early stories, resemblance to narrators of, 114
eighth grade *Oliver!* tryout, 94
Fine Arts Work Center fellowship, 32, 33
first book published and reviewed, 260
first book submission, 34
first poem, 31
first stories sent to literary magazines, 34
first unpublished novel, 126
fourth grade teachers (dreadful), 102
graduate school, Iowa Writers' Workshop, 21, 90, 124, 221
identity as a writer, 3, 8, 29, 30, 43, 273
inoculated by pencil, 61, 102
karaoke and, 88, 92, 223
library science studies/library jobs, 2, 33, 35, 242, 244, 246
Modern American letters, feelings about, 199, 200
narrative choices, 10, 161
playwriting class, 159
preferences for art, 7–9, 100
progress in her writing, 230
published and unpublished works, 3, 260–265
publishing houses and editors, 264–266
rejections and, 34, 141, 264–268
scrap files, 216
self-loathing method for getting work done, 27, 33, 93
short story writing, 78
university position and campus office, 33, 38, 245, 246
titles of her books, 242

writing habits and rituals, 25, 26, 29, 33, 36, 38, 58
writing poetry, 159, 160
writing process for, 36, 38–40, 42–47, 58, 88, 116–124, 156–158, 161, 162, 164, 176, 183–185, 269
a year of writing almost nothing, 25
See also language, *specific elements of fiction*
McCracken, Elizabeth: as teacher of creative writing, 98, 142, 225, 226, 229, 246
box of index cards, and a lizard, 219
"Buck up, for God's sake," advice, 256
fondness for students, 270
goal with students, 15
habitual manuscript marginalia, 272
mistaking a student for a stranger, 123
moats around her writing time and, 246
question on the first day of class, 150
reading student work, 33, 225, 246, 248, 273
rules for or notions about writing fiction, 7, 17, 18–19, 179, 194
starting out as a teacher, 145
students' influence on, 145, 275
student's novel brought to class too soon, 211
students' overuse of favorite words, 192
student's query about atmosphere, mood, and tone, 195
success of former students, 16, 211
teaching in MFA programs, 100
unkindest critique by, 91
writing as unteachable, 279
years as a teacher, 15
meaning, 21, 91, 140
changed or lost meanings of words, 182
explanatory conjunctions or adverbs and, 168
humor as a kind of meaning, 202
italics and, 171, 172
meaning without a soul, 19
paradox of, 112
reader's job to find, 112, 167, 202
space breaks and, 167
visual appearance of text and, 9, 170
when adverbs are most useful, 178
metaphors, 12
getting better at writing them, 188
labored or automatic, 189
for language's relationship to fiction, 190
McCracken's, for fiction, 271
McCracken's, for her imagination, 117
Michelangelo, 206
mirrors of life, 82
mood, 195

N

narrative choices, 46,
- deliberate or unaware, 47, 87
- effects of different decisions, 47
- flashbacks, 82–85
- forks in the road, 55
- making a decision and going forward, 55, 56
- McCracken's decisions and inspirations, 10, 161
- period of time the story covers, 81
- setting, 87
- tense, 34, 52, 75–78, 87
- warning about, 87
- who's telling the story and how, 47–73

narrators, 7, 47–73
- first-person narrator, 48, 51, 53–55
- first-person narrator, writing a biography for, 57
- first-person narrator and indirect constructions (filtering verbs), 59
- first-person plural narrator, 63
- internal monologue, 51
- second-person narrator, 49, 64
- third-person narrator, 49, 58, 65–69
- third-person narrator and child characters, 67
- third-person narrator with multiple points of view, 67, 71–73
- third-person narrator with multiple points of view, guideline for, 73
- "unreliable" narrator, 54
- using all points of view, 49, 50

nonfinito, 277

notes, note-making and notebooks, 38–40

novels, 124, 210–21
- characters and, 125
- comparisons or metaphors for, 158, 214
- compressing time in, 81
- a draft like a chess set, 218
- events in chronological order, or not, 81–85
- as fluid, not tectonic, 83
- period pieces, 204
- popular titles, 242
- prologues in, 171
- revisions and drafts, 213–218
- rules and, 18, 19
- the subject of most novels, 81
- when to let someone read it, 210, 211
- *See also* drafts; revisions

O

Oliver! (musical), 94, 95
- "Where Is Love?", 95

outlines, 43, 45, 164
- McCracken's post-draft outlines, 164

Out-of-the-text writing, 57

Oxford English Dictionary, 11

P

paragraphs
- length, 165
- lyric essay or internet paragraphing form, 165
- movement forward and, 183

Paris Review, The, rejection note, 141
past tense, 75–77
perfectionism, 255
physicality (of characters), 133–141, 143
  body as the apparatus of plot, 148
  defined, 137
  estrangement from the body versus awareness of, 137
  gesture and, 138
  how to avoid characters being stuck in their heads, 134–136
  putting yourself in a character's body, 137
  visualization practices for, 137
  yanking characters into their physical selves, 143
playwriting, 159
plot, 46, 150, 151, 154, 252
  active and emotional plots, 151, 154
  body as the apparatus of, 147, 148
  character and, 158, 160
  childhood and, 149
  consequence and, 156
  constructed around travel, 155
  default, average plots, 140
  defined, 150, 151
  event and, 151
  interference among characters and, 218
  McCracken's changing view of, 156
  McCracken's fiction and, 150
  novel draft that lacks plot, 218
  secrets and, 153
  what to do if plot eludes you, 154, 173
poetry, 117, 159
  lessons about writing fiction from, 160
  McCracken's first poem, 31
  McCracken's persona poems, 159
  as multidirectional, 159
  reading and listening to, as inspiration, 117
  visual appearance of, 170
present tense, 7
  interesting present tense, 86
  in short story taken from McCracken's second unpublished book, 78
  as a narrative choice, 87
  in real life, 76
  qualities of, 75–78
  tension and, 87
  writers' affinities and, 78
prologues, 171
publishing, 239, 241
  failure following success, 250
  fashions in publishing and book titles, 242
fear of humiliation and, 238
  habit of comparison, 233–235
  low (or no) expectations for, 241
  McCracken's editors, 264–266
  McCracken's emotional responses to her published books, 260–263
  McCracken's first book, 260
  rejections, 34, 141, 225, 250, 264–266
  success and, 259

fear of humiliation and (*cont.*)
terror before a book's publication, 238, 239
writing a book you don't believe in and, 250
punctuation, 166, 167, 169
bad habits and, 169
chapter breaks as, 164
for dialogue, 176
exclamation points, 166
meta punctuation, 166
music of prose and, 169
space breaks, 167
style and, 165–167

R

readers. *See* audience
realism
in fiction, 82, 128
fiction vérité, 128
reference books, 11
Oxford English Dictionary, 11
Roget's Thesaurus, 11
rejections, 34, 224, 250, 264, 265
by *The Paris Review*, 141
resilience, 249
revisions
accidental patterns and, 117
adverbials and, 180
butter cow analogy, 206
cutting words, 168, 184
how to know when you're done, 247
insurmountable problems surmounted, 218
language choices, 183
McCracken's recent novel, major cuts in, 162
novel revision, 213–217
post-draft outlines, 164
scrap files and, 216
short-story revision, 209
walking away from a book, 248
See also drafts
Roget, Dr. Peter Mark, 12
Roget's Thesaurus, 11, 12
rules for writing, 17, 18
absolutes that may be helpful, 7
as devoid of meaning, 21
from the Iowa Writers' Workshop, 21–23
"kill your darlings," 21
McCracken's three "rules," 19
"real writers write every day," 23, 24, 29, 32
"show, don't tell," 21, 71
story's own rules and, 18
throwing away rules, 18
"write what you know," 21

S

scaffolding, 163
scatological humor, 141
setting, 4, 87, 146, 252
being specific and idiosyncratic, 204
characters' beliefs and, 146
as context, 146
defined, in relationship to character, 144
time period, 71
Shakespeare, William
Hamlet, 179

short stories, 124, 125, 207–209
characters and, 125
compared to a family photograph in an antique store, 158
digression in, 207
as dioramas, 207
drafts, 207
emotional heart of, 207, 209
flashbacks and, 82
plot and, 151
process for writing, 124
revision of, 207
subtlety in, 207
titles, 242
why a short story fails, 18
structure, 46, 163–170
anything visual and, 170
chapter breaks and, 164
scaffolding and, 162
subconscious structure, 164
suspense as, 163
time as, 85
style, 180
chapter breaks and, 164
cutting explanatory conjunctions and, 168
double spacing and, 167
editing and, 183
exclamation points, 165
good language as economical, 183
italics and, 171
paragraphs and, 165
personal, 91
space breaks, 167
See also language
subconscious mind and writing
character creation and, 117
good writing day followed by nightmares, 185
structure and, 164
tips for awakening imagination/the subconscious, 117
suspense, 81
as structure, 163

T

talent, 252–254, 259
as static, internal, inadequate, 254
technique, 15, 49
tense as a narrative choice, 47, 51, 75–77, 86
theme, 4, 74
time, 45
as subject of novels, 81
compressing time in novels, 81
as structure in novels, 84, 87

See also flashbacks; past tense; present tense
time period (setting), 71, 146, 204
titles, 242
generation of, 173
tone, 195
what it is, 195
travel
plot structure and, 154
while young, and later in life, 155

U

"unreliable" narrator, 54

V

verbs
  attenuation, 183
  dialogue attributed by, 176
  filtering verbs and indirect constructions, 59
  seems, 179
  weakened, in fiction, 180
  See also adverbs
voice, 90, 91, 99
  analogies for, 92
  style and, 91
  what it is, 91

W

Winchester, Sarah, and the Winchester Mystery House, 271, 277
writer's block (any type), 173
writing
  age/stage of life and what you write, 19
  ambition as everything, 19
  animating spirit of, 108
  answering the question: "how will you get work done," 27, 32, 38
  appetite for work and, 254
  a book of your heart and, 15, 274
  computers and, 39, 173
  cure for all writerly maladies, 231
  cyclone fence metaphor, 187
  depth in, 203
  desire for approval, 95, 97, 98
  difference from ballet, piano, chemistry 19, 24, 48
  different writers, different advice, 18, 37
  discovery of what works, 25, 37
distractions and, 34–36
  durability of the written word, 118
  focus on the process, 19
  getting started, 44
  great writers who repeatedly write the same book, 19
  how to use advice about writing, 9
  identity as a writer, 29, 30
  "I'll show them" as motivation, 31
  improvement versus change as a writer, 71
  lifelong learning and, 277
  losing the habit of comparison, 233, 234
  making the process a contest with your friends, 26
  "no binary question is interesting," 29
  nonfinito and, 277
  no prodigies and no masters, 275
  notes, notes on anything handy, and notebooks, 38–40
  passion and soul, 19
  perfect as uninteresting, 255
  perfectionism, 173, 217, 255
  personal style or voice, 90–92
  plodding versus whipping the wind through your hair, 32
  progress in, 230
  risk and fear of failure, 258
  self-doubt and, 185, 249

stopping and starting again, 24
the subconscious and, 117, 164, 185
as synesthetic, 170
travel (dislocation) and, 155
use of hatred or love, 9
as weightlifting, 109
what to write for, instead of approval, 98
See also fiction

writing life, the, 3
association with other writers, 21
bad habits romanticized, warning, 19
the bullheaded writer, 19
careers ruined by jealousy, 236
distractions and, 34–36
experiencing the world as a writer, 29
failure following success, 250
fiction writers and karaoke, 88
lack of parental support as a gift, 186
the lucky break and, 251
need for resilience, 249
oddness, obsessions, and, 19
self-loathing and writers, 27
a steady job and its pitfalls, 245, 246
success/eventual reward, 259, 263
superstitions and, 33
work habits and self-discipline, 19, 36, 254
writing in company, 36
See also publishing